# JERSEY ALPHABET

GW00707412

*Cover: Bathing belles at Havre des Pas Swimming Pool;
Overleaf: Advertisement for Jersey Airways, c. 1936*

# HOW TO REACH JERSEY BY AIR

A FOUR ENGINED 14 SEATER "EXPRESS" AIR LINER OVER BOULEY BAY, JERSEY, AFTER A FLIGHT OF ONLY ONE HOUR FROM SOUTHAMPTON.

# JERSEY AIRWAYS L<sup>TD</sup>

IN ASSOCIATION WITH
THE SOUTHERN AND GT. WESTERN RAILWAYS

## BOOKING OFFICES

## DAILY SERVICES
## TO JERSEY

| LONDON | SOUTHAMPTON |
|---|---|
| SINGLE 59'6 | SINGLE 35'- |
| RETURN 99'6 | RETURN 60'- |

| DETAILS ON REQUEST | • AIRSEA TICKET INTERAVAILABILITY<br>• BAGGAGE IN ADVANCE FACILITIES<br>• SERVICES TO GUERNSEY AND ALDERNEY<br>• THROUGH TICKETS AVAILABLE FROM GLASGOW, LIVERPOOL, MANCHESTER BIRMINGHAM, E<sup>TC</sup> | APPLY ALL TOURIST AGENCIES |

### LONDON
CHANNEL ISLANDS AIR LINES
VICTORIA RAILWAY STATION
S.W.I. 'PHONE. VICTORIA 5692/5.

### SOUTHAMPTON
SOUTHAMPTON AIR PORT
'PHONE EASTLEIGH 87243,

### JERSEY
AIRWAY HOUSE, ST. HELIER
'PHONE' JERSEY 1221.

**45,000 PASSENGERS** WERE CARRIED IN 1934 AND 1935 **WITHOUT INJURY**

# JERSEY
# ALPHABET

Compiled and presented by
## John Le Dain

**SEAFLOWER BOOKS**

Published in 1997 by
SEAFLOWER BOOKS
An imprint of
EX LIBRIS PRESS
1 The Shambles
Bradford on Avon
Wiltshire

Design and typesetting by Ex Libris Press

Cover printed by Shires Press, Trowbridge, Wiltshire

Printed and bound in Britain by
Cromwell Press, Broughton Gifford, Wiltshire

© John Le Dain 1997

ISBN 0 948578 84 X

*The author wishes to thank Clifford Du Feu, retired Jersey solicitor,
for his help and advice with a number of entries in* Jersey Alphabet

*To the memory of Fred Manning*

# CONTENTS

5

*Note: Cross references are indicated in bold type.*

# A

## ABREUVOIR
A roadside watering place, mainly for animals, not to be confused with the generally more elaborate **lavoir**, or place for washing clothes, but with which the *abreuvoir is* sometimes incorporated.

## ADVOCATE
Jersey **law** has its basis in ancient Norman law and has evolved over the centuries to serve the particular needs of the Island. Advocates correspond to Barristers at Law in England; they have to pass an examination in Jersey law and hold a degree. Solicitors, formerly known as *écrivains*, practice law in the Jersey courts but do not plead at the Bar, a privilege reserved for Advocates in the Royal Court and the Magistrates Court. English solicitors have no jurisdiction in any of the Jersey Courts of Justice.

## AIR TRANSPORT
The first aircraft to touch down in Jersey came from France: in 1912 the French Aero Club organised a race from St. Malo to Jersey and back – four aircraft landed on the beach in St. Aubin's Bay, refuelled and returned. Similarly, when Jersey Airways was formed in 1933, in the absence of a permanent runway, its De Havilland Dragon took off from West Park beach bound for Portsmouth. Notwithstanding the inconveniences of a timetable which depended on the state of the tide, the service proved an immediate success.

In the following year services were begun to Southampton

and London. Just as the Jersey **Chamber of Commerce** had lobbied successfully for a new harbour in the previous century, so it urged the States to finance the building of an airport – it was opened in 1937. (Alderney, most difficult of approach by sea, was the first Channel Island to open an airport – in 1935). Bigger planes were now able to serve Jersey and the volume of passengers and air freight grew steadily until the Germans arrived in 1940. Military operations encouraged development of the airport, including its use by fighters to escort German bombers en route from France to attack England. Since the War the airport has been continuously upgraded until, in 1995, a major rebuilding programme was begun.

Air transport is now more important than ever, with large numbers of aircraft movements daily, to serve an ever-growing range of international destinations. The only complaint, and it would seem to be a fair one, is directed at the high cost of air fares between Jersey and the mainland, relative to many more distant lands.

**ALMANAC**
Or, to give it its present full name, *Jersey Almanac and Trades Directory*, is an annual publication which features a wealth of current information concerning life in the Island. Subjects covered include meteorology, office holders in government and law, members of various professions, data on the major industries of finance, tourism and agriculture, and clubs and organisations. A list of businesses, classified by subject, is followed by the largest section: a complete list of islanders, parish by parish, street by street. The *Almanac* concludes with a series of detailed maps and a gazetteer. Overall, it provides a source of detailed information on many aspects of Island life; old editions are an invaluable source of reference to anyone researching family history.
*Jersey Almanac, Michael Stephen Publishers,*
*PO Box 582, Five Oaks, St. Saviour, Jersey*

## APPLE CRUSHER

This object, often mistakenly referred to as a cider press, may sometimes be seen as the centrepiece of a Jersey front garden – a massive wheel set in an equally massive circular trough, all hewn from granite. The apples were tipped into the hollow and the wheel harnessed to a horse which pulled it round and round to pulp the apples (when the pulp was transferred to the press).

The frequent appearance of these old apple crushers in Jersey provides a clue as to the former importance of the cider industry. The heyday of apple-growing and cider-making was two and three hundred years ago, when apple trees occupied up to 20% of arable land. The aspect of the countryside must have been vastly different from today – imagine looking across the countryside at blossom time! Correspondingly huge quantities of cider were produced, the great bulk of which was destined for home consumption!!

Cider drinking gradually fell out of fashion and, by the beginning of the present century, the industry had shrunk considerably. However, town dwellers were once accustomed to head for the country at potato picking time to help gather the crop and, at the end of each thirst-inducing row, to avail themselves of a swig of refreshing cider, a barrel of which was customarily provided by the farmer.

## ARCHITECTURE

The architecture of Jersey was habitually regarded, by writers and observers from England, as inferior and unworthy of notice. Baron von Aufsess, one of the Commandants of Jersey during the Occupation, was that puzzling contradiction – a Nazi with finer feelings. He wrote as follows in his *Occupation Diary:*

> 'The local people are curiously insensitive to the beauty of their island. The capital town of St. Helier is a good example of this, with its utilitarian buildings and uncompromisingly commercial air, devoid of artistic merit or natural affinity with the surrounding countryside.'

Then, after the Occupation, along came Joan Stevens of the Société Jersiaise and her monumental work, *Old Jersey Houses.* The first volume covers the period 1500-1700 and appeared in 1965; the second, covering from 1700 onwards, was published in 1977. This detailed and invaluable study traces the evolution of Jersey architecture through the centuries.

The earlier houses were four-square, thatched and solidly built of local granite. They had many characteristic features, such as the *tourelle*, or winding staircase, housed in a mini-tower, part of which often projects from the rear wall; the great round arches, often incorporating dated keystones, on which their owners lavished attention; the carved and inscribed door and window lintels and gable stones. Inside there was the enormous fireplace, with its projecting corbels supporting a massive stone (or occasionally timber) lintel.

After about 1700, Jersey's house-builders or, rather, the increasingly wealthy families who demanded new houses, became aware of current fashion, viz. for a symmetrically proportioned house in what became the Georgian style, with spacious rooms, high ceilings and tall windows. Although granite remained the universal building material, the masons who had shaped the tough native stone were called on less and less as the arch and decorated door and window surrounds fell from favour (with the exception of the increasingly popular **marriage stone** over the main entrance).

A great building boom, particularly in a fast expanding St. Helier, took place throughout the Victorian period, with impressive crescents and terraces mainly built to house the large numbers of newly arrived **residents**. After 1700 the sash window became universal, as did the dormer window. There is a characteristic of both which is special to Jersey. The two main components of the sash window are typically painted in contrasting colours – the frame a dark green, or blue, or red, and the sliding windows white. This two-tone paintwork is commonplace in Jersey, at least on those buildings where the original sash windows have not yet been replaced by new, plastic, double-glazed units, which are always boringly white. The dormer windows very often have the projecting side panels glazed in order to maximise the passage of light into the dark attic rooms and to provide a sort of mini-greenhouse.

The single common feature of Jersey's buildings which provides a welcome visual unity, not only between diverse structures of different periods but also between them and the landscape, is the use of **granite**. It is true that elevations are often rendered and painted but the underlying granite is, reassuringly, never far from view.

Exterior decoration – in the form of various mouldings – developed to an elaborate degree in late Victorian and Edwardian times. Today such façades are often picked out in a dazzling variety of colours to give a most exuberant overall effect, like a wedding cake.

One of the comparatively unsung attractions of Jersey architecture is the wealth of good buildings in the Art Deco style of the inter-war years. There are many examples dotted around town and, indeed, all over the island, e.g. the old Playhouse in

Bath Street and the Forum Garage at First Tower and the splendid house Les Lumières (1933) in Route Orange, St. Brelade.

After many years of tireless lobbying by individuals and groups intent on preserving the best of Jersey's built environment, agreement was finally reached in 1996 to list some 2,000 structures deemed worthy of protection. This was followed by a publication entitled *Jersey's Lost Heritage*, presenting a selection of 'before and after' photographs to show the generally adverse effects which piecemeal redevelopment has had on the character and appearance of St. Helier during the past quarter century.
*see also* **TOWN**

### The ARTS

Here are a couple of quotes from visiting Englishmen in the last century:

> 'The arts of life are low among them, or they are too parsimonious to avail themselves of them.' (1830)
> 'It is to be regretted that there is not a little more enthusuasm on the subject of the fine arts.' (1862)

You still hear such sentiments expressed today, although States funding of the Jersey Arts Centre and the many expanding branches of the Museums Service in recent years has done much to counter the Island's reputation as a desert of art and culture. Only twenty years ago it was a difficult task to find good original paintings of the Island; now there are a number of galleries which offer a wide choice of high quality work from a mainly local stable of artists. The Jersey Arts Centre puts on an extremely varied programme, is particularly strong in the performing arts and encourages home-grown talent at every opportunity, as does the annual Jersey **Eistedffod**.

So why the former reputation, at least partly based on fact, that Jersey was uninterested in the arts? It may have been partly due to the low church influence, which scorned all kinds of music and dance as frivolous and ungodly activities. And it may have been partly due to the fact that Jersey Norman-French, the native tongue, was never a written language but merely spoken. There is no doubt, though little evidence, that there was a tradition of folk song and dance and of story-telling but that creeping Anglicisation and non-conformist ethics conspired to suppress it. And, perhaps too, there was a tendency among the true Jersey folk to keep their culture to themselves, as a buffer against the onslaught of an alien culture.

Jersey has had its share of great painters – John Le Capelain, who painted the Battle of Jersey, the Ouless brothers and, most famously of all, Sir John Millais, a former President of the Royal Academy, who painted **Lillie Langtry** as 'A Jersey Lily'. It is interesting that these Jersey artists developed their talents in exile and not in the land of their birth. At least a partial exception was **Edmund Blampied** who, after pursuing an artistic career in London, returned to Jersey in 1938 and spent the rest of his life working in the Island.

What seems so regrettable is that there was never a great writer to capture and record something of the life of old Jersey – a sort of Thomas Hardy of the Channel Islands. The nearest we have is the Guernseyman G.B. Edwards whose book and life's work, *The Book of Ebenezer Le Page*, published in 1981, is the greatest work of fiction produced in and about the Channel Islands though, of course, set in Guernsey. No doubt the language difficulty provided an obstacle to wider literary markets. French would have had little sale in England and, to France, the Channel Islands were alien and often hostile, even if the true islanders had been sufficiently at home in English to have used it as a medium for creative writing.

# ❋ B ❋

## BAILIFF

The Bailiff of Jersey is both chief magistrate and President of the **States**. The office-holder is thus the head of civil affairs and presides over the States Assembly (where he may speak but cannot vote) and the **Royal Court**. He also presides over the Electoral College which elects the **jurats**. The Bailiff selects the lieutenant-bailiff (i.e. his deputy) from among the jurats.

Lord Coutanche was one of Jersey's longest serving bailiffs and held office from 1935, through the difficult Occupation years, until 1962. More recently, Sir Peter Crill left office in 1995 after a decade of service and has been followed by Sir Philip Bailhache.

Formerly, the office of Bailiff was secondary to that of **Governor** but it has since grown in importance. Though appointed by the Crown, the Bailiff has traditionally been the defender and upholder of the special immunities and privileges of Jersey. Indeed, there have often been bitter struggles between the Bailiff and the Islanders, on the one hand, and the British Government on the other.

## BAILIWICK

For the purposes of administration, since 1485 the Channel Islands have been divided into two Bailiwicks – Jersey, which includes the offshore reefs of the Ecréhous and the Minquiers, and Guernsey, which includes Alderney, Sark, Herm and Jethou. Each

Bailiwick has its own constitution and legal system (and Alderney and Sark have their own subsidiary constitutions).

## BANNELAIS

This Jersey-French word refers to road scrapings – traditionally leaf mould, weeds and horse manure – which are heaped up under the hedges, collected and auctioned annually at parish meetings. *Bannelais*, therefore, is an example of recycling rooted deep in Jersey's history and in the character of a people always intent to make the most of what nature has provided and to keep their surroundings tidy. Once a valuable compost, one wonders whether the road sweepings of today, which must contain a fair proportion of ring pulls, filter tips and fragments of non-biodegradable plastic, as well as being impregnated with the toxic fumes of vehicle exhausts, is quite such a coveted commodity.

## BATTLE OF FLOWERS

Undoubtedly and deservedly Jersey's best known annual fixture, the Battle of Flowers was first held in 1902 to celebrate the Coronation of King Edward VII, then held each year until the First World War. It was revived in 1928 and celebrated annually under the auspices of the Royal Jersey Agricultural and Horticultural Society in their Springfield Showground. The Occupation stopped the fun but, once again, peace time witnessed its revival. The Battle has been held annually since 1951, on the last Thursday in July, in Victoria Avenue.

In recent years, the Battle of Flowers has become a misnomer since the closing 'battle', when the elaborate and painstakingly arranged flower-decorated floats were ripped apart in an orgy of destruction by spectators and participants alike, has ceased to be a part of the proceedings. The risk of minor injury at the 'Battle' of Flowers may have abated but a sedate affair it certainly is not. The floats grow more ambitious as each year passes; they are prepared by the parishes, by local clubs and societies and, increasingly, by commercial concerns.

The flowery floats are interspersed with marching bands and the whole procession takes best part of an afternoon to pass up and down Victoria Avenue. A recent and welcome development has been the advent of the moonlit parade, i.e. the same thing in the cool of the evening. This can provide a refreshing alternative to standing all afternoon under a hot sun. And the firework show staged from Elizabeth Castle is an added bonus.

Finally, it is remarkable how the weather always turns out fine for the Battle of Flowers; even when the morning is dull and cool, the clouds invariably part to allow the sun to shine down and spotlight the floats to full effect.

## BEACH CAFE

An unsung and underrated feature of the Jersey scene, but a wonderful institution nevertheless. Like public conveniences, the beach café is never far away, so that one may not be kept waiting for a refreshing cuppa, a cooling ice cream or a replenishing bite.

The Jersey beach café is, generally speaking, a splendid example of individual private enterprise – each has its speciality and personal touch. Beach cafés are often sited in makeshift wooden structures, lovingly repaired and repainted between seasons. Some are mobile and are housed in former ambulances and other suitable vehicles. Others may have been converted from buildings which had a previous function. For example, the Millbrook Café in St. Aubin's Bay occupies a former railway station on the St. Aubin's Railway, while the Gunsite Café at Beaumont is housed in an old German gun emplament. Still others are purpose-built, such as the West Park Café, the cafe at St. Catherine's or the large establishment at Le Braye.

Some have profitable sidelines other than catering; for example, water-skiing at La Haule and sub-aqua at Bouley Bay, but all provide food and drink of some description, as well as sun cream, Jeffrey Archer novels, prawning nets and all the other paraphernalia which seems essential to a day on the beach. The best beach cafés are wonderful – the Driftwood Café, at the little frequented Archirondel on the east coast, offers an imaginative menu and a selection of home-made cakes which may be enjoyed *al fresco* together with a delightful view across the beach and down to the sea. The El Tico at St. Ouen's is a good place for food and views, and the Blue Peter at Rozel another which affords a lovely view, as intimate as El Tico's is panoramic. Highly recommended is Colleen's Café at Grève de Lecq where the cream teas are delicious in every detail. And, if you are into nostalgia, don't miss the Casino Café beyond it – the interior, as well as the menu, has an atmosphere redolent of the 1950s.

## BEAN JAR
... or Bean Crock. This simple country dish is a traditional Jersey meal which appears to have made something of a comeback in recent times.

A mixture of dried beans are left to soak overnight. They are placed in an earthenware jar, covered with water, brought to the boil and simmered for several hours. Onions, herbs, and a pig's trotter or lump of pork are thrown in to add some interest and a good, solid, nourishing if unsophisticated meal is the result. We are told that, traditionally, the bean jar provided a breakfast dish specially on Sundays.

## BERGERAC
A town and wine producing region on the River Dordogne in south-west France which has no obvious connection with Jersey, though it is the name taken by the hero of the eponymous and long-running TV detective series. Set largely in Jersey, 'Bergerac' was launched in 1981 and proved a sufficient success to warrant further series which were filmed and broadcast each year until 1991, when the last episode was screened.

The actor John Nettles played the detective who, in the earlier series, was employed at the fictitious 'Bureau des Etrangers'; he appeared in every episode that was made so that John Nettles was Bergerac in every sense. The series took full advantage of Jersey as a film set and almost every nook and cranny of the Island appeared at some stage.

For many who know Jersey, 'Bergerac' proved essential viewing, not so much for the story lines (which were often so contrived as to lack all credibility), but for glimpses of the beloved isle, particularly the early episodes in which Jim lived in an old stone house in the as-yet-unflooded Queen's Valley, where he was shacked up with the delectable Francine. Watching 'Bergerac' became a sport in which the object was to be the first to recognise all the bits of the Island which appeared on screen. And it was fun to spot the occasions when the director had taken liberties with the set – for example, when Bergerac, in pursuit of a villain in town, drove into Fort Regent tunnel only to emerge on the Five Mile Road!

John Nettles, during his years in Jersey, evidently developed quite an affection for the Island, so much so that he did not give up easily when his application to purchase a property was repeatedly turned down by the authorities; he eventually won his case. In 1988 he published his first book, *Bergerac's Jersey*, in the modern vogue of celebrities writing books about the landscape with which they are associated through their work. Interestingly, Nettles tackled his subject parish by parish in a not unsuccessful attempt to draw out the essential characteristics of Jersey's twelve constituent parts. The book benefited, too, from the inclusion of a dozen of Michael Richecoeur's etchings and many illustrations from the hand of **Edmund Blampied**.

Four years later, in 1992, Nettles' second book on Jersey was published, this one entitled *John Nettles: a Personal View of the People and Places*, which was certainly a personal, indeed quirky selection, and included accounts of key figures in Jersey's history, of the Occupation years and a chapter entitled 'Jersey Killings' which includes an account of the then unsolved Newall case.

John Nettles/Jim Bergerac has lent his image and support to a number of local causes, most notably in publicity for the Jersey Gold Centre, where his famous Triumph Gloria open-top car may be seen. The legend also lives on in the naming of the Bergerac Hotel at Portelet and the Bergerac Wine Bar in St. Helier. The 'Bergerac' series was generally regarded as good publicity for Jersey, though one has often heard the remark from people that, having seen the TV programmes, they would not dream of spending their holidays in such a crime-ridden island.

## BLACK BUTTER

... or *Le Nière Beurre* in Jersey-French is spread on bread, like ordinary butter. This Jersey dish probably dates from the seventeenth century; its main ingredient is apples, so it is not surprising that black butter fell from favour with the demise of apple-growing. But, like many old ways, its preparation and consumption has seen something of a revival.

Indeed, the preparation is, and probably always was, as much of an attraction as the end result. Black Butter Night was preceded by the communal peeling and chopping of a quantity of apples. The result was shovelled into an enormous brass preserving pan and balanced upon a trivet with a fire beneath. A gallon of cider was added to every 70lbs. of apples – maximum capacity, 10 gallons. The apply mixture was kept on the boil all day – friends and neighbours arrived to help with the constant stirring of a wooden spoon. This process went on throughout the night and was accompanied by general merrymaking and, no doubt, a fair amount of cider drinking. Finally lemon, spices, sugar and sometimes liquorice were added ... as dawn broke the steaming mixture thickened, grew dark and the cooking was complete. Everyone was given a supply of black butter to take home.

## Edmund BLAMPIED (1886-1966)

Blampied is, by now, probably and deservedly, Jersey's most famous artist. We are told that he was the son of a Jersey farmer who, as a child, spoke little English; indeed, until he took art lessons in St. Helier at the age of fifteen, Edmund had never seen a town. Soon after this he transferred to London, where he subsidised his studies by contributing topical pen and ink sketches for the *Daily Chronicle*. He took up etching in 1913 and in 1925 won a Gold Medal for lithography at the Paris International Exhibition.

During the Occupation he lived at St. Aubin where he designed six Jersey postage stamps and Jersey banknotes and, later, one of the Channel Islands liberation stamps. He was an etcher and lithographer and drew and painted in pencil, oil and water colour; his favourite subjects were landscapes and figures. Indeed, he often combined the two by portraying the Jersey peasant farmer at work in his fields or, most famously, on the beach collecting *vraic*.

Blampied illustrated many books include *Peter Pan, Black Beauty* and R.L. Stevenson's *Travels with a Donkey*. But perhaps the most interesting and singular of all is *Jersey in Jail* published in 1945, a volume which is as attractive in presentation as it is unusual in content.

Almost any work of Blampied's is now sought after and samples may be seen in some of St. Helier's galleries. There is no doubt that there are Blampied drawings and paintings hanging on living room walls throughout Jersey which are unrecorded and otherwise unknown. He surely deserves his own gallery, perhaps in a converted barn somewhere in the country; some of those local guardians of Blampied's work may be persuaded to lend them for exhibition. Here we could feast our eyes on his sometimes comical, sometimes touching, sometimes daringly impressionistic but most often quintessentially Jersey view of the world.

## BRANCHAGE

More correctly referred to as *Visite du Branchage*, this is an ancient Jersey custom carried out annually on a parish basis. It consists of an inspection of the roads by the parish authorities – the owners of the land bordering the roads are responsible for seeing that trees and hedges do not obstruct the movement of traffic. Each year, as the time for the *branchage* approaches, there is a flurry of cutting and trimming along the known route of the parish inspection. If there are infractions, fines are collected on the spot. The *branchage* is very much a living tradition and is an effective way of keeping parish thoroughfares fully accessible.

## BRETONS

Inhabitants of Brittany (*Bretagne*) in north-west France. The Bretons have little connection with the Normans who occupy that part of France on the opposite side of the Bay of Mont St. Michel and, by extension, little to do with Jersey. They have their own customs and way of life and, more significantly, they speak their own language, a Brythonic tongue akin to Welsh and Cornish and quite unlike Jersey Norman-French.

However, because Brittany was relatively poor, the younger people from the farms were traditionally drawn to Jersey to tend the fields. Until quite recent times, several thousand souls would arrive in St. Helier Harbour each year in time to sow the seed potatoes. They would stay to dig them later in the season, then immediately plant the tomatoes and tend them through the summer months until ready for picking.

A colourful description of the annual Breton invasion is given in R.M. Lockley's book, *The Charm of the Channel Islands*, published in 1950:

'The arrival of these (mostly young) French workers at St. Helier harbour in the St. Malo boat is an amusing and animated sight. Each carries a knapsack, and many have bicycles. Many of the men have the broad, short-bladed, straight-handled scythe of France over one shoulder. All are chattering volubly, mostly in French patois or the Breton tongue, and they are hailed fraternally by their employers, or, more extravagantly with the traditional three kisses, one on both cheeks and mouth, by friends and relatives who have either arrived earlier or spent the winter at work in Jersey. These workers are on contract with farmers: they will dig his potatoes at so much per vergée, and cultivate, stick, tie and tend his tomatoes at so much per thousand plants. They live in outbuildings and barns, provide for themselves and seldom take an hour off, wet or fine; unless it is to go to St. Helier on Saturday afternoon to meet friends.'

The Clarendon Hotel in Market Street was a venue popular with the Bretons; on Saturday afternoons the air was raucous with the shouts of the French workers and one could scarcely see across the back bar for the blue haze produced by Gauloise cigarettes. The only English phrase to be heard was the oft-repeated demand for 'a pint of beer'.

Neighbouring Hilgrove Street was known as French Lane and these few streets adjacent to the market formed the hub of French life in Jersey, at least on Saturdays. During the 1930s, following an agreement with the British Government, Jersey agreed to take unemployed from the mainland to work in the fields. The results were not very satisfactory. Brittany is no longer the impoverished backwater it was and the Bretons come no longer: they have been replaced long since by the Portuguese.

*Opposite: Illustration drawn c. 1890 depicting Bretons gathered on the corner of Hilgrove Street ('French Lane') and Bath Street. Note the traditional dress of the women, including the sabots, or wooden clogs. The sign above the corner indicates the Soleil Levant– the pub here is still known as such – and the proprietor: P. Coquet.*

# C

## CABBAGE

The Jersey cabbage, of gigantic proportions, was once a not uncommon sight in the countryside, and a source of pride among Islanders – it was comforting for a small island to lay claim to the biggest of something, if only the unexciting cabbage! Here is a quote from David Ansted in 1862:

> 'A particular kind of cabbage (*chour-cavalier*, or great cow cabbage) is cultivated both in Jersey and Guernsey, but chiefly in the former island. The stalk of this plant attains almost the dimensions of the trunk of a tree. Stalks, perfectly straight and hard, are frequently obtained upwards of ten feet in length. The leaves of these cabbages are constantly stripped as they become large, either for feeding cattle or packing butter, and the plants are left growing with a small crown at the top like palm trees. The stalks are ultimately taken up, and are serviceable either for palisades or pea-sticks, the stouter ones being manufactured into walking-sticks.'

Not many indigenous folk songs survive in Jersey, but Raoul Lemprière, in one of his invaluable books on the Channel Islands, refers to one inspired by *le chour:*

*J'ai perdu ma femme, en pliantant des chours.*
I have lost my wife, while planting cabbages.

Older readers will recall the walking sticks made from the stems, varnished and sometimes adorned with a Jersey penny in their head, which were once a much sought after souvenir and sold in shops in St. Helier. An old guide book refers to, 'The craving evinced by visitors for these sticks is known as "the Jersey fever".'

## CAESAREA

The Latin name for Jersey, used by the Romans, though some authorities dispute it; Jersey was certainly also known to the Romans as *Andium*.

## CENTENIER

Jersey's parish-based honorary **police** force is headed by the **Constable** who is assisted by **centeniers** and **vingteniers**. The centenier is so called because he was originally charged with the well-being of a hundred families. To be a centenier may be an honour and a route to higher office but it is also a considerable responsibility. Centeniers are on duty as parish policemen according to a rota and every case taken to the police court is in the charge of a centenier who presents it on behalf of the Constable of his parish.

## CHAMBER OF COMMERCE

Jersey Chamber of Commerce has a particular claim to fame: founded in 1768, it is the oldest in the English-speaking world – just one of the Island's many pioneering achievements.

The origins of the Jersey Chamber of Commerce lay in the conflict between the established order and the rising merchant class and its challenge to the hegemony of the hereditary ruling families. In addition, the British government of the time did not much respect the Island's traditional rights and the red tape it imposed in order to control trade with North America frustrated Jersey enterprise. Local merchants organised themselves into a

Chamber of Commerce so that, collectively, they might have a stronger voice. Interestingly, while this new body was granted a Charter of Incorporation by the British Government, it met opposition from the States, who saw the Chamber as a threat to its own authority. Nevertheless, it fought successfully against repeated attempts by the British Treasury to establish custom houses in the Channel Islands and maintain the Island's tax privileges.

The Jersey Chamber of Commerce has always striven to ensure the commercial and trading health of the Island, notably the development of St. Helier's Harbour; after almost a century of agitation, it was finally enlarged in the nineteenth century.

The Jersey Small Business Association was set up in 1993 to represent the interests of small businesses following the difficulties experienced during the recession of the early 1990s This new organisation enjoys the full support of the Chamber of Commerce.

## CHANNEL ISLANDS

Besides Jersey, there do exist a number of other Channel Islands, namely Guernsey, Alderney, Sark, Herm, Jethou and Brecqhou plus an assortment of islets, reefs and rocks.

Guernsey is little more than half the size of Jersey with a proportionately smaller population; Alderney is smaller again with a little over 2,000 people; Sark has about 550, Herm a handful of souls and Brecqhou the itinerant, mysterious, millionaire twin brothers Barclay. In other words, Jersey's population easily exceeds that of the other islands put together.

It seems remarkable how utterly different the islands are in appearance and character. St. Helier is fast-paced and the most urbanised community; indeed, the first task after arrival at the Harbour is to negotiate a six-lane highway and an underpass, having been greeted by an ever expanding area of reclaimed land, a fuel store, power station and the more distant prospect of downtown office blocks.

Guernsey, by contrast, is like a bypassed English country town, with a decidedly provincial air. Nevetheless, Jersey has been the more successful in protecting its countryside from the developers. Alderney is rather bleak and windswept, the least French though the closest to France, and suffers a slightly oppressive atmosphere on account of the layers of fortifications which are everywhere evident – but St. Anne's is a most charming place. Sark is a natural fortress, surrounded by grim looking rocks and with a main street which looks like somewhere in the Wild West or the Australian outback. The island is very beautiful and, because of the absence of traffic, thoroughly relaxing, though you must watch out for the bicycles, which can be pretty lethal. Herm is a gem – Jersey Tourism's former publicity slogan which claimed Jersey to be 'Britain's South Sea Isle' would more aptly be applied to Herm.

Jersey, though the largest Island, lies somewhat apart from the rest – a full 18 miles from Guernsey. Both main islands, not surprisingly, share much history in common but it is a fact that, politically and culturally, each Island has evolved down the centuries to exhibit quite distinct features. The two islands took opposite sides in the Civil War – Jersey was Royalist and Guernsey Parliamentarian – and seem to have been rivals ever since.

Guernsey sailors considered it unlucky to mention Jersey while at sea, even if bound for Jersey, while a proverb in both islands has it that anyone who marries a partner from the other Island will never live at ease. Locals do visit their sister Island, usually for the day, but the commonly heard remark is that the other Island is not as beautiful and it's good to be back in one's own island.

Efforts to promote the interests of the Islands seem to be made individually rather than on a cooperative basis – take the major industries of agriculture, tourism and finance as examples. If Jersey and Guernsey were closer physically they might be stauncher allies – who knows? A favourite badge and bumper sticker in Guernsey declares, 'GUERNSEY – THE THINKING MAN'S JERSEY', suggesting either that Jerseymen are intellectually challenged, or that those who choose to visit that Island are a few brain cells short of the average. But one cannot help noticing, on the Channel Islands-bound ferries, for instance, how the ramblers with rucksacks and birdspotters with binoculars tend to disembark at Guernsey, while the noisy young fellows at the bar who have been doing their best to get plastered since leaving the mainland are remaining on board until they reach Jersey. One elderly Jerseyman I know, who visits Guernsey regularly in his capacity as a sales representative, assures me that he has nothing against Guernsey people but that they have a terrific inferiority complex regarding Jersey (implying, therefore, that Jersey is greatly superior!)

## CHARACTER OF THE PEOPLE

'The typical Jerseyman today, in his sturdy independence, his self-reliance, his shrewdness at a bargain, his tremendous industry, his reticence, his thrift, is almost the exact counterpart of the peasant farmer on the opposite Normandy coast.'

So wrote Jersey's great historian, G.R. Balleine, in 1951. Indeed, many observers of the Jersey character trace a continuity from the plundering Northmen, through the Normans who founded a considerable empire, to the inhabitants of a still distinctive province of France and their sea-girt cousins in 'Les Iles Normandes'. Yet, often, these same observers note certain negative aspects of the Jerseyman's legendary independence, industriousness and integrity, namely, his parsimony, or stinginess. Here is Henry Inglis, writing in 1834:

> 'That love of acquisition and a strict frugality forms a strong trait of Jersey character is undeniable.'

And David Ansted in 1862:

> 'The people, as may be imagined from the returns of the savings banks, are in the habit of hoarding, and are exceedingly careful in regard to money matters. Even those who have secured incomes sufficient to render them independent are generally parsimonious.'

Jersey folk may be shrewd but it is difficult to recognise that meanness of character to which earlier observers so often allude. It is surely most visitors' experience that Jersey folk are welcoming and generous to a degree which surpasses the average mainlander. It may be the case that the period of enforced isolation and genuine hardship during the Occupation years had an effect upon the Jersey character. Having little money to spend and even less to spend it on perhaps resulted in a happy-go-lucky and even spendthrift reaction during the post-war boom.

*Peasant of St. Ouen; mid-nineteenth century.*

But the Jersey love of independence is perhaps more enduring. David Ansted wrote in 1862 as follows:

'These islanders are Normans, but Normans of the old school – Norman freemen before they were Norman barons and vassals of the crown, retaining the northern love of independence, and not at all the Gallic tendency to depend on the fostering hand of a central government.'

And here, nearly a century later, is R.M. Lockley, the farmer, naturalist and writer, who lived at Fliquet during the years after the Liberation:

'The islanders originated from Norman stock of the pioneering freeman type, and they have never lost this strong feeling of independence. There is certainly much in their present bearing that confirms this inherited strength of character, which is marked by a love of individual enterprise, ability to work hard, a liking for autonomy and freedom of speech, and a veneration for their own language, laws and ancient customs. As in many other small isolated communities, their hospitality is abundant, yet the stranger is soon aware of the tenacious nature of their own family connections, and it is a long time before the settler in their midst is accepted as one of them.'

How qualified has this portrait become fifty years later? Can it be said that Mr Ansted's appealing metaphor still rings true:

'The islanders are like their own granite: sound, tough, hardy and not easily sculpted or worked into soft artistic forms.'

## CHRISTIANITY
The view opposite of the Royal Square, the ancient heart of St. Helier – once the market place and, in 1781, scene of the Battle of Jersey – depicts the statue of George II in the foreground, the former States Chambers on the left and the squat tower of the Parish Church, the oldest building in town, in the centre distance.

If you turn your back to this view and walk a short distance along Queen Street, you may look along the straight reach of Halkett Place – leading towards the 'New Town' which developed after 1800 – to the imposing façade of the Wesley Grove Methodist Church. Its exuberant paint scheme and illuminated cross put one more in mind of a Catholic church in southern Europe, perhaps Malta, than the plain, unadorned style which one is more likely to encounter in a non-conformist place of worship. But look beyond and to the left of the Wesley Grove façade and you will espy the tall and slender spire of St. Thomas Roman Catholic Church.

These three very distinctive buildings – the Parish Church of St. Helier, the Wesley Grove Methodist Church and the Roman Catholic Church of St. Thomas – represent Jersey's three major strands of Christianity: Anglican, Methodist and Roman Catholic. What is the story behind this profusion of faiths?

The early inhabitants of Jersey were converted to Christianity by a succession of Celtic and Roman missionaries, firstly

St. Marculf, who is attributed with converting Jersey in 538AD (some years before St. Augustine arrived in Britain) and later St. Brendan (St. Brelade) and St. Helier who reached Jersey in 555AD.

The Normans became enthusiastic church builders throughout their empire. We are told that the original core of the Parish Church of St. Helier was a simple chapel probably thrown up in the ninth or tenth century – rough, sea-worn boulders make up the outer wall of what now forms the chancel and suggest that once it was close to the beach. The interior is surprisingly small but is well cared for and full of history and interesting memorials; nevertheless, it has a light and cheerful atmosphere and imparts the sense of a living place of worship.

Jersey remained in the Diocese of Coutances in Normandy until the Reformation, which reached the Island via France, and met with little resistance. All manifestations of the old order were swept away: wayside crosses were cut down, chantry chapels converted into dwellings and the parish churches stripped of all adornment, including their altars, fonts, statues, wall paintings and stained glass windows. Indeed, Catholicism was deemed illegal. The rectors of the new regime were mostly French Protestants in Presbyterian Orders; Calvin's Prayer Book became universal.

But Jersey folk, with their own language, traditions and independent spirit, would not surrender completely to Calvinism and were influenced by rival aspects of Protestantism for years to come. In 1499, Henry VIII bribed the Pope into transferring the Channel Islands to the Diocese of Winchester but, for another fifty years, the Bishops of Coutances exercised effective authority over church affairs in Jersey. In 1620, James I took advantage of a lingering resistance to Calvinism and moved to impose Anglicanism on the Island. He abolished the Presbyterian form of Church government; the Jersey church was placed firmly under the control of the Bishop of Winchester and a French translation of the English Prayer Book was to be used in every church.

Even so, Jersey's independence was never completely suppressed. There was a brief resurgence of Presbyterianism later in the century under Oliver Cromwell but Anglicanism remained in the ascendant until the Methodist Movement reached Jersey in 1774. John Wesley visited the Island in 1787 and his journal records the events:

'Monday 20 August
We took ship [from Guernsey] between three and four in the morning, in a very small inconvenient sloop, and not a swift sailer, so that we were seven hours in sailing what is called seven leagues. About eleven we landed at St. Helier's ... I preached to an exceeding serious congregation.

Tuesday 21 August
We took a walk ... had a view of the whole island, the pleasantest I ever saw ... the little hills, almost covered with large trees, are inexpressibly beautiful.

Wednesday 22 August
In the evening, the room not containing the people, I was obliged to stand in the yard. I preached and spoke exceeding plain; even the gentry heard with deep attention.

Thursday 23 August
I rode to St. Mary's, five or six miles from St. Helier's through shady pleasant lanes. None at the house could speak English. but I had interpreters enough ... The houses here are exactly like those in the interior parts of Wales, equal to the best farmers' houses in Lincolnshire and the people in general are far better behaved than our country farmers in England.'

John Wesley spent barely a week in Jersey but seems to have

made a considerable impact and to have been gratified at the reception his message evinced among all classes of people. Perhaps the moral certainties of Methodism struck a revivalist chord with a people which had, by and large, welcomed the Reformation and, in particular, its Calvinistic interpretation.

In fact there was opposition to Methodism. Believers had a long struggle to convince the authorities that Methodist members of the Jersey Militia should be excused drill on the Sabbath. But all obstacles to their freedom were eventually overcome and the Methodist cause flourished for generations to come – chapels were erected all over the Island and Methodism became the prime denomination of the indigenous Jersey folk. Until quite recent times, the Methodist network consisted of the English circuit, i.e. the town churches, and the French circuit, the country chapels, in which the preaching and hymn singing were performed in French. Methodism still exerts a powerful, if waning, influence on the Jersey character and way of life. The recent extension of Sunday pub opening hours was hotly contested by the Methodist lobby, as is, at the time of writing, the proposal to build a casino in the Island.

Meanwhile, in France, Roman Catholics, with whom the French Royalists identified, were undergoing harassment and persecution and some 7,000 fled to Jersey in the 1790s for sanctuary and, in 1803, they were permitted to open a chapel in Castle Street. At the turn of the nineteenth century many teaching and nursing orders, such as the De La Salle Brothers and Little Sisters of the Poor, found refuge from the anti-clericalism which existed in France. The French Roman Catholic influence eventually found expression in the impressive church of St. Thomas where a tablet commemorates, 'Retablissment du Culte Catholique à Jersey par Mathieu de Gruchy et les Prêtres Français Emigrés'. Inside, the elegant granite stonework complements some dazzling stained glass. A Sunday Mass in French is still held, to which has been added one in Portuguese. St. Thomas is currently one of eleven Roman Catholic churches in Jersey.

Wesley Grove, notwithstanding its attractive and beckoning façade, is difficult of access. Indeed, no regular services are now held.

Today, happily, the ecumenical spirit flourishes and all three major strands of Christianity in Jersey exist in harmony. In 1840, a guide book writer passed the following comment:

> 'The observance of the sabbath is strictly maintained in Jersey, and the inhabitants generally may be designated a church going population.'

Today, the parish churches, country chapels and various Catholic churches, for the most part, attract healthy congregations, at least compared to the mainland.

But let us return to our starting point: the Parish Church of St. Helier. One noticeable feature which has been added latterly are the boldly marked out parking places adjacent to the church walls – uncompromisingly designated for the Verger, the Dean, the Organist, etc. Perhaps Jersey Christians should coin an eleventh Commandment: 'Thou shalt not covet thy neighbour's parking place.'

## CLAMEUR DE HARO

An ancient Jersey custom which is not only picturesque but may be effective in righting a perceived wrong. Rollo was the great tenth century chief of Normandy; the word 'Haro' is believed to be a corruption of 'O Rollo', the cry originated as a plea to Rollo for swift and certain justice. The *clameur* must be uttered in the presence of two witnesses, including the Attorney General who represents the public, and the aggrieved party cries, 'Haro! Haro! A l'aide, mon Prince, on me fait tort', which means, 'Help! My Prince, I am being wronged.' This has the effect of an immediate injunction restraining a person from committing an alleged wrong until the appropriate court has been able to consider the matter and pass judgment.

The most famous *clameur* was raised at the funeral of William the Conqueror. When building St. Stephen's Abbey in Caen, William had demolished several houses without paying any compensation to their owners. After his death, as his coffin was being lowered into his grave in the Abbey, one of the dispossessed householders raised a *clameur* and his claim was allowed. The *clameur* was abolished in Normandy but survives in Jersey. It is still occasionally raised in modern times, though severe penalties await anyone who wrongfully makes the appeal.

## COLOMBIER

In feudal times, it was the privilege of the **Seigneur**, or Lord of the Manor, to have a *colombier* or dovecot in which to keep pigeons to provide the household with meat during the winter. Important persons other than seigneurs were later allowed to do likewise and the holes cut into the front walls of certain old Jersey houses date from this period. There are eleven purpose-built colombiers which survive today; those at Samares and Hamptonne are accessible examples and are certainly impressive structures.

## CONGER EEL

Together with the **ormer**, which is a mollusc, the conger eel is possibly the sea creature most commonly associated with Jersey. It can grow to enormous proportions – up to seven or eight feet in length and as thick as a man's thigh.

From early times, at least until the onset of the

Newfoundland cod fishery, in which Jerseymen were so closely involved, the conger eel was exported, either dried or smoked, to ports all round the French and English coasts. A typical Jersey dish is conger soup, made out of the head of a conger eel which is boiled in milk and to which is added marigold petals and leaves, though this last ingredient may not be familiar to many local cooks.

## CONSTABLE
Sometimes also referred to as 'Father of the Parish', the Constable is the parish representative in the States and head of the honorary **police** in his parish. He is assisted in his duties by his **centeniers** and **vingteniers**. The office of Constable has long been held in much respect – witness the sometimes elaborate memorials to former parish constables, or *connétables*, which may be seen around the Island.

## COTIL
Pronounced 'co-ty', is one of those **Jèrriais** words which survives in common usage in the Island today. A *côtil* is cultivated land on a steep slope which is most often planted with potatoes. If the *côtils* face south or west then they will produce the earliest crops so are much prized, even though their considerable angle makes working them very laborious. Farmers on the mainland would rarely be bothered with such difficult land but the cultivation of *côtils* has always been a feature of Jersey farming, where every patch of fertile soil is valued.

## COW
Jersey's single greatest claim to fame must surely be its cow, specimens of which have been sent to all corners of the world and herds of Jersey cows are established in the most unlikely places. Here is a description of the beast by David Ansted in 1862:

'The breed of horned cattle has long been known, and is in many respects remarkable. The important peculiarities are the small size and delicate frame of the animals, the large quantity and rich quality of the milk they yield, and the yellowness of the fat and of the butter made from the milk ... Although very small, many of the cows are remarkable for symmetry; and they rarely show a vicious temper. They have a fine-curved taper horn, a slender nose, a fine skin, and deer-like form.'

The Jersey cow bears a close connection with the cattle of the coastal districts of Normandy and Brittany. However, no live cattle have been allowed into Jersey since 1789 and two centuries of inbreeding has resulted in an animal with its own special characteristics; these tend to be lost in cows bred outside the Island, so that traditionally there has been a healthy trade in the export of live cattle.

From the farmer's point of view, the Jersey cow suits local conditions – it has a modest appetite and is reckoned to be the most economical converter of rough herbage, producing milk with a very high butter-fat content. To make the best use of this efficient beast, the Jersey cow is sometimes tethered in order to control her grazing and to make efficient use of every patch of grass, though today electric fences are more likely to be the means of controlling a cow's grazing. The writer and farmer, R.M. Lockley wrote that, 'The treasure highest in the Jerseyman's estimation is his cow, she seems to be the constant object of his thoughts and attentions.'

In this time of agricultural decline, the number of herds is decreasing and those that remain are becoming larger to make them economically viable. The Island herd currently numbers around 4,000 and it is noticeable how less often one encounters cows in the countryside today. Jersey milk, with its high fat content, is not the attraction for the health-conscious consumer that it once was.

The noble image of the Jersey cow has suffered somewhat of late with the appearance of the slightly vulgar 'Lillie the Cow' – the latest attempt by Jersey Tourism to promote the Island as a holiday destination. It remains to be seen whether this cavorting comic-strip creation will prove efficacious but it will certainly do nothing to maintain the dignity of Jersey's greatest claim to fame.

## CRAB

The common crab – the big, broad-backed pink ones you see on fishmongers' slabs – is known in Guernsey as *chancre* (anglicised to 'chankers') but in Jersey as the Guernsey crab, owing to the greater size and more frequent occurrence which the species attains in that island – a rare instance of Jersey bowing to the superiority of the sister island. One explanation of the lesser size of Jersey specimens is offered in the following account, written by David Ansted in the last century:

'The reason for the disparity probably lies in the large number of poor French families living in Jersey, who scour the shore unceasingly, and to whom nearly every living thing from the size of a winkle upwards, represents food.'

The same writer observes that the common green crab, which is generally believed to be inedible, was indeed also once eaten:

'The green crab, generally so despised, is in Jersey consumed eagerly by the poorer among the islanders.'

Today the spider crab is much sought after in Jersey (and on the Continent) though it is generally not eaten on the mainland. It is, indeed, many islanders' favourite variety and the ritual of sitting at the kitchen table to reduce a spider crab to a heap of edible meat, on the one side, and of shattered ectoderm on the other, is one indulged in by many a spider crab fancier. The intricate shell case and numerous legs are picked over to yield up every shred of delicious meat. But here is Mr. Ansted again:

'Cartloads of the large spider crab may sometimes be seen in summer in the markets. On a bright summer day at spring tide even women and children are constantly to be seen tramping up and down in shallow water at low tide feeling for their prey with their feet.'

One hopes they had some sort of protection from spider crabs' claws!

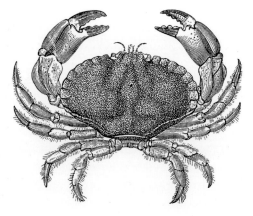

## CRAPAUD

is the French word for toad and is one of those old words which has entered common usage; it refers to the Jerseyman who is known, especially by the Guernseyman, as a 'crapaud'. There was even once a Jersey newspaper entitled *The Crapaud*, first published in April 1835. The Jersey toad was much celebrated on account of its great size and ubiquity. Indeed, the species formerly grew to a far greater size than its cousins in France or England. David Ansted, writing about the middle of the last century, not untypically blames the French for the decline of the crapaud:

> 'It [the crapaud] was until recently extraordinarily abundant even on the outskirts of town, but since the introduction, in large numbers, of farm labourers from Brittany, it is getting more and more scarce, the Breton labourers having a great horror of this most useful and inoffensive little animal, and never failing to destroy every one they come across.'

The Jersey *crapaud* survives, though but a shadow of its former self.

# D

## DEAN

The Dean, head of the Anglican Church, is appointed by the Crown. He is the President of the Ecclesiastical Court and appoints two Vice-Deans from among the eleven assessors who are rectors of the eleven other parishes of the Island and is automatically a member of the **States** Legislature, but may not vote.

## DEPUTY

Twenty-nine deputies are elected from the **parishes** to sit in the **States** of Jersey – ten representing St. Helier, five St. Saviour, three St. Brelade, two each St. Clement and St. Lawrence and one each the seven remaining parishes.

## en DESASTRE

This phrase (every bit as bad as it sounds) relates to bankruptcy in Jersey and affects only personal and movable estate. It is a procedure widely used and operated by the Viscount, the executive Officer of the Royal Court. In case of insolvency, when real estate is concerned, the procedure since 1880 takes the form of a *Dégrèvement*, or discumberment of mortgaged property or insolvency of the proprietor. The earlier procedure was known as *Décret*. By a modern statute the equity, if any, in the property after payment of all claims whether secured or otherwise, is returned to the debtor in bankruptcy.

## DUTY-FREE

Because of Jersey's low taxes, relative to the mainland, the attractions of duty-free goods have traditionally been a great attraction for visitors to the Island. Duty-free is, in fact, something of a misnomer, because the States of Jersey levies a tax on such luxuries as alcohol and tobacco products, and the differential between local and mainland rates has been narrowing considerably in recent years. Not so many people smoke these days and, with the competitive pricing of wines and spirits in UK supermarkets, it is now hardly worth the trouble of purchasing 'duty-free' alcohol as you leave the Island. And, compared to the practically limitless allowances available to citizens of the EU from countries like France, where drink and tobacco are so much cheaper, the relative attractions of Jersey now seem rather insignificant in this respect.

A range of other goods may be cheaper in Jersey, including jewellery, perfume and all items subject to Value Added Tax, which does not apply in Jersey. On the other hand, the absence in the Island of the 17.5% VAT which is levied on most goods and services in the UK is often gobbled up, partly or wholly, by the cost of shipping goods to Jersey, or so local retailers claim.

Marks and Spencer, for example, impose a 5% surcharge on all food items while reducing VATable items, such as clothes, by 10%. It's a swings and roundabouts situation, certainly, but one is left to conclude that, as far as indirect taxation is concerned, there remains little practical difference between Jersey and the mainland, and the attractions of duty-free goods are pretty much a thing of the past, though there was a time when it was an irresistible game to attempt to smuggle duty-free goods to England.

# LARBALESTIER'S

## ESTD. 1813

## THE ORIGINAL JERSEY EAU de COLOGNE

### Pharmacist, Perfumer & Photographer

### 2 & 3, CHARING CROSS

#### 41, COLOMBRIE.

# E

## ECREHOUS

Pick a clear, calm day and a high perch to look out towards France from the north-east corner of Jersey and you will see, about half-way between yourself and the French mainland, a string of rocky islets bearing what appears to be a considerable mass of old buildings. In certain conditions it almost looks like a higgledy-piggledy street afloat at sea. This is the Ecréhous, a group of islets whose sovereignty has long been a bone of contention between Britain and France, and where incursions by French fishermen, even to the point of raising the tricolour, occur to this day. British ownership was confirmed by the International Court of Justice in 1953; the rocky reef forms an offshore domain of the parish of St. Martin.

The main islets are Maître Ile, Marmoutier and Blanche Ile. There is evidence that the Ecréhous have been inhabited since prehistoric times though the first reference to them was in 1203. There are the ruins of a Priory on Maître Ile, a customs house displaying the arms of Jersey on Marmoutier and a number of houses and cottages frequented by visiting yachtsmen and fishermen. Jerseymen discovered the reef's potential first for *vraic* gathering and burning and, later, as a convenient base for smuggling.

*Opposite: Attractive advertisement in the art deco style of the 1930s for locally made Eau de Cologne, once a favourite duty-free item.*

In the last century a Jerseyman, Philip Pinel, lived there for nearly fifty years and became known as 'King of the Ecrehous'. When Queen Victoria visited Jersey in 1857, he sent her a gift of fish in a basket which he had fashioned from dry seaweed. It is not recorded whether Queen Vic was amused by this fishy gift, but she did return the compliment by sending him a coat.

## EISTEDFFOD
is a word borrowed from the Welsh and was adopted by Samuel Falle, Dean of Jersey (1906-37), who was inspired by the ancient annual event which is held each year in the Celtic provinces of Wales, Cornwall and Brittany. Since its Jersey incarnation, in 1908, the Eistedffod has become very much a part of the annual calendar. The performing arts lie at the heart of this home-grown festival, including speech and drama (in English and French), singing and music, staged in the Opera House, as well as two-dimensional art, crafts and photography. The Eistedffod includes the widest possible range of age groups, with the close involvement of schools and youth groups. Another interesting feature is La Séthée Jérriaise, an entertainment conducted in Jersey Norman-French.

The following is a quote from the 1996 programme of events: 'The aims and objectives of the Jersey Eistedffod are the advancement of artistic, educational and cultural activity by stimulating and encouraging by competition, performance and exhibition the practice and appreciation of arts and crafts in Jersey and the preservation of the Island's language and heritage.'

## EVENING POST, JERSEY
Founded in 1890, it has now overtaken the French-language *Chronique de Jersey*, which was published from 1814 to 1917, as the Island's longest lived newspaper. Its current circulation is around 24,000 copies, six days a week, which is said to represent the highest per capita circulation of any newspaper. It has a tabloid

format and is quite a chunky publication, most often numbering 48 pages but sometimes many more, besides the supplements on various topics which frequently appear.

Lead stories are always of local interest, as are the first few pages, though the world beyond Jersey is allocated a couple of pages. There are a lot of feature articles which provides the reader with interesting, in-depth material on all manner of Jersey people and their enterprises. The Letters page is invariably entertaining – readers are never shy to express an opinion and a lively correspondence often follows some controversial decision by the States. There is a page full of notices and reports – weather and tides; Centeniers on Duty; shipping movements; official notices concerning planning applications, bankruptcies, etc, under the heading 'Jersey Gazette', and so on. Small ads and the 'hatch, match and dispatch' columns (births, marriages and deaths) take up several pages and each issue is rounded off by reports of local sporting events.

The *Evening Post*, or *JEP*, is most definitely a Jersey institution and certainly lives up to its proud claim to be 'at the heart of Island life.' It remains a mystery why it doesn't appear at breakfast rather than midday. Successive editors have claimed it represents the opposition in a society where there is no party politics. In the last century, Jersey was riven with party politics and each of the two opposing parties had its mouthpiece in a newspaper. But the end of party politics has not resulted in a withering away of democracy – as the leaders and letters pages of the JEP bear witness.

The *Jersey Evening Post* moved from its Bath Street premises to a new, spacious premises at Five Oaks in 1977, though a small office in maintained in town, and was early in the field with computer-aided production. Informative, entertaining and well presented, the *Jersey Evening Post* has deservedly won official recognition as an excellent newspaper.

*Jersey Evening Post, PO Box 582, Five Oaks, St. Saviour, Jersey.*

## F

## FAMILY HISTORY

Jersey folk are undoubtedly proud of their inheritance and many carry on the family names of their Norman ancestors (see SURNAMES). Two excellent organisations offer assistance to anyone seeking to discover their Jersey forebears – the **Société Jersiaise**, in whose library is a card index referring the enquirer to a wealth of material, much of it the product of earlier enquirers researching the same name. In addition, the Channel Islands Family History Society (CIFHS) issues a list of members and their interests and publishes an excellent journal as well as occasional books. A good starting point is the booklet *Family History in Jersey* (see page 125 for details).
*CIFHS , PO Box 507, St. Helier, Jersey.*

## FEUDAL SYSTEM

The Channel Islands are often referred to, disparagingly and out of ignorance of the facts, as outposts of the feudal system. The Norman Empire which, after 1066, included England, was organised along feudal lines, that is, the Duke of Normandy parcelled out his newly conquered possessions amongst his supporters, in recognition of their past and future loyalty, thereby granting them considerable powers in their new domains. Jersey was divided into fiefs; the four great fiefs of St. Ouen's, Rozel, Trinity and Samares were reigned over by their **Seigneurs** who had the right to flog, imprison and put to death their tenants. In addition, there were well over a hundred smaller fiefs which, in turn, were divided into sub-fiefs, though with reduced powers.

Right down to the eighteenth century, tenants had to perform all sorts of onerous duties for their Seigneur. In England, the industrial revolution and the mass movement of population from the countryside to industrial centres led to the inevitable decline of the feudal system – embodied in the Lords of the Manor, directly descended from their Norman ancestors. In Jersey, other sources of prosperity, most notably sea-borne trade and commerce, resulted in a shift of economic and political power away from the feudal overlords.

In the present day, though shadows remain, Jersey is no more a feudal system than rural England. Indeed, it is arguable that Jersey's is the more democratic system! Sark, however, with its Seigneur and *tenantes*, remains the Channel Island where the feudal system is much more than a vestige. Even there, few can remember the Seigneur flogging, imprisoning and putting to death his subjects, though Dame Sybil Hathaway certainly brooked no nonsense from the Germans during the Occupation.

## FLAG

The Jersey flag is a red cross on a white background – actually the cross of St. Patrick – which was mistakenly adopted in 1841. The Island colours are, correspondingly, red and white. The official flag of the Lieutenant-Governor is a Union Jack with the arms of the bailiwick at its centre. This is flown from the flagstaff in the grounds of Government House when the Lieutenant-Governor is in residence, from the bonnet of his car and on any ship on which he is embarked.

## FLORA & FAUNA

Because of its geographical isolation, the flora and fauna of any island invariably features some unique species and Jersey is no exception. Successive Ice Ages led to fluctuations in climate and changes in sea level which, in turn, meant that Jersey was sometimes attached to the continental land mass and at other times an island. Plants and animals, including man, migrating westwards across Europe, would sometimes have reached Jersey and, at other times, have been unable to do so. Even today, there is ample evidence that Jersey was once much larger – tree stumps at St. Ouen's exposed at certain states of the tide show that a coastal forest extended westwards; beds of peat containing beetle cases and vegetable remains may sometimes be observed beneath the shingle at Fliquet on the east coast.

Peculiarities of Jersey fauna include a wood mouse and a bank vole which are slightly different from their respective mainland counterparts, whilst the strikingly coloured Jersey tiger moth, Jersey grasshopper and lesser white-toothed shrew do not occur elsewhere (though the last is found on Sark, where it is thought to have accompanied Jersey settlers in the fifteenth century). Jersey, like Brownsea Island, is a stronghold of the red squirrel, which has been all but eradicated from mainland Britain by the voracious grey squirrel, though it is likely that it was introduced to the Island in the nineteenth century, as was the hedgehog. Rabbits were introduced by the Normans as a source of food and are now the Island's most common wild mammal.

The Jersey toad, or *crapaud*, was once more common than it is today, while the only species of frog – the agile frog (a particularly good jumper) – is struggling to survive the pressures of pollution and a growing human population. There are no poisonous snakes but slow worms are often abundant and exhibit a different colouring to their English cousins. The green lizard is a striking animal; the sandy reaches between the road and sea-wall at St. Ouen are a good place to spot these handsome creatures, while the ramparts of Gorey Castle support a colony of wall lizards.

Bird life is represented by a dazzling variety of species, because Jersey provides such a range of habitat, particularly in its sea shores with their enormous tidal movements. Some bird species have increased dramatically in numbers in recent years, most notably (many would say infamously) the herring gull, or sea gull. Natural scavengers, herring gulls traditionally found food on the beaches but, with people creating so much edible rubbish, the herring gull has moved into town, nesting on rooftops and raiding dustbins. They are unashamed opportunists – a gull has been observed to swoop down and take a bite out of a hot pasty as its owner raised it to his mouth.

The cliffs, hedgebanks, stone walls, valleys and marshes of Jersey provide a variety of habitats for wild flowers, whilst the extensive area of sand dunes at St. Ouen comprise one of the most important such ecosystems in Europe and a base for many specially adapted plant species, some of which are so small that the keen botanist must get down on all fours and employ a magnifying glass. Some of Jersey's wild flora represent garden escapes, while other species have arrived as seeds with birds or were transported by sea to take root in the Island's generally favourable and frost-free climate. As a result, there are species originating from the Iberian peninsula, from islands off Africa and from the continent itself, as well as from the Caribbean.
*see also* CRAPAUD, HYDRANGEA

**FORT REGENT**
Occupies Mont de la Ville overlooking St. Helier and was traditionally a place of refuge in times of attack. The summit was levelled in 1785 to provide a drill ground for the Town Militia and, in the process, an ancient dolmen was unearthed. In 1804, during the Napoleonic Wars, the Crown acquired the hill in order to construct Fort Regent, completed in 1814 and named after the then Prince Regent, the future George IV. Its massive granite block walls now enclose a Leisure Centre which was developed in the 1970s and which offers facilities for a wide range of sports and entertainments.

# G

**GENEALOGY** *see* **FAMILY HISTORY**

## GOVERNMENT

Within the British Isles but not a part of the United Kingdom, self-governing and not represented in the Houses of Parliament at Westminster, independent in matters of law and finance (though any new laws must be ratified by H.M. Government in Council) but reliant in international affairs and for defence purposes on the U.K. and not (yet) a full member of the European Union, an understanding of Jersey's governmental system takes some grappling with.

Prior to 1485, the British Crown appointed a Warden of the Channel Isles. Thereafter Jersey and Guernsey had their own governments and became separate administrative units. All principal officers are appointed by the Crown, viz. the **Bailiff** (President of the **States**), Deputy Bailiff, Attorney General (who acts as Chief Prosecutor), Solicitor General and **Dean** (head of the Anglican Church).

Government is carried out by means of a number of standing committees (currently 26 in number, though soon to be reduced), each of which has its particular area of administration. Many of these committees, such as Agriculture and Fisheries, Education, Finance and Economics and Housing, are household names in Jersey and regularly make headlines in the *Jersey Evening Post* (where, oddly, they are always referred to in the plural, such as 'Education promise more schools'). Their sometimes controversial policies are often the subject of fierce debate and members, especially the Presidents, thereby earn fame (or notoriety).

Far from being an outpost of **feudalism**, as Jersey is sometimes caricatured from the outside, it surely possesses, in many respects, a greater degree of democracy than the mainland. There's no doubt that the Island contains a higher proportion of elected officers and representatives per head of population than almost any other democratic community – at both States and parish level – the latter including the honorary **police**.

Whilst the past twenty years has witnessed the erosion of the welfare state and decline of government intervention in every field of activity in Britain, Jersey now enjoys comparatively favourable levels of States funding for those in need and for a broad range of worthwhile public projects. The States take seriously its responsibility for the provision of housing to local people – witness the two-tier market, the subsidising of new building and the extension of States loans at favourable rates of interest. All this is happening while, on the mainland, the public housing stock has largely been sold off and the market left to its own devices. It may not yet be quite a socialist paradise ('The People's Republic of Jersey'?) but Jersey is a beggar-free zone, unlike much of the mainland, largely thanks to its concerned and effective government and the undoubted advantage accruing from its offshore status.

**GOVERNOR** *see* **LIEUTENANT-GOVERNOR**

## GRANITE

'Jersey may be described as a block of granite, roughly nine miles by five, tilted to catch every ray of the southern sun ... the impression left on the visitor is that wherever he goes he meets granite, sometimes red, sometimes blue, sometimes grey, sometimes purple – granite cliffs, granite castles, granite churches, granite farms, granite piers and pavements.'

So said the great Jersey historian, G.R. Balleine, in a book he published in 1951. It is true that Jersey is all but synonymous with granite but, in fact, the Island is composed of a variety of rocks, though the majority, like granite, are tough crystalline rocks of igneous origin. Igneous rocks include all those which were formed from once molten material, either within the earth's crust or on the surface, having been extruded from volcanoes or cracks in the earth's crust. The deeper the molten rock, the more slowly it cools, and the larger the crystals which form. Some of the coarsest crytalline rock in Jersey may be found in the south-west, from the Noirmont headland round to Ouaisné. Here the 'granite' is composed of large crystals of colourless quartz and bright pink felspar.

Generally speaking, granite and granite-like rocks comprise the rocky headlands of the north-west and south west, i.e. those bits of the Island which bear the full force of the Atlantic, as well as much of the low-lying south-east, including enormous areas of rock which are exposed there at low water. These rocks exhibit a wide variety of colours and textures, depending upon the particular balance of minerals present and the nature of its formation. Sometimes the granite is classified as gabbro or diorite, or one of a score of other rock-types, and sometimes it is interrupted by a crystalline rock of volcanic origin, such as andesite or rhyolite.

Two other main rock types occur: in the north-east, including

St. Catherine, Fliquet and Rozel, there occurs the Rozel Conglomerate, a puddingstone rock composed of fragments of earlier rocks mixed up in a once molten matrix. This is not a particularly beautiful stone but provides an interesting contrast to the outcrops of 'pure' igneous rocks more typical of the Island. It is not much used as a building stone, except in the sea walls around that north-east corner.

The Jersey Shale Formation is a relatively soft and easily eroded rock which gives rise to the low-lying and deeply indented bays of St. Ouen and St. Aubin. Unlike all other Jersey rocks, this shale is of sedimentary origin, i.e. it was deposited on the sea floor and later compacted and transformed into solid rock. The shale is best observed at St. Ouen where it gives rise to all those smooth grey stones below the sea wall which accumulate towards the northern end of the bay.

In addition to the underlying rocks, Jersey possesses deposits of much more recent origin, in particular, the wind-blown sand which forms the mountainous dunes of Les Blanches Banques at St. Ouen, and the wind-blown loess originating in the last Ice Age, a finely textured deposit which lays the basis of Jersey's generally fertile and easily worked soil.

Jersey's older buildings are typically constructed of blocks of pink-hued granite. Nevertheless, some of the less visible parts of buildings as well as garden walls and outhouses are randomly constructed from the first stone most convenient of use – from a cutting in the nearest hillside, or even from the beach.

Current regulations dictate, quite rightly, that new buildings are at least faced with granite and that existing granite structures are protected. It is surprising, perhaps, that much of the granite used in Jersey was imported from the Minquiers and the Ecréhous; where large quantities of stone are required, transport by sea was always more economical than overland. All current granite extraction takes place at Sorel on the north coast.

Amazingly, it is not an easy task to acquire a gravestone made from Jersey granite – you are likely to be informed that you can have one made of granite from Cornwall or India, but not from Jersey, which seems ridiculous in an Island built on the stuff.

At one time the most productive and famous quarry in Jersey was at Mont Mado in St. John. Stone from Mont Mado – of a pink tint and capable of taking a high polish – was used for the Victoria Embankment in London.

It is puzzling that more is not made of Jersey granite, in all its attractive variety, on a small scale. Why can't we buy polished pebbles or blocks, probably more for decorative use (though one could think of practical uses), but worthwhile nevertheless. The Jersey mason's craft was much to the fore in the last century and evidence is everywhere to be seen – from massively large-scale set pieces like St. Catherine's Breakwater or the States Buildings in Royal Square to the parish churches and the numerous and carefully wrought examples of 'street furniture' like **lavoirs**, parish pumps, parish boundary stones, and so on.

It is surprising, perhaps, that as well as extensive stone quarrying, Jersey at one time enjoyed a considerable brickmaking industry. By 1853 exports of Jersey bricks reached 2,000,000; Jersey sailing ships bound for the Newfoundland fishing grounds carried bricks as ballast. The industry ended in the 1950s.

**GREEN LANES**
The 1990s has witnessed the emergence of the system of Green Lanes, where priority is given to walkers, riders and cyclists and motor vehicles are encouraged to restrict their speed to 15 mph. St. Peter pioneered this scheme and it has since been taken up by most other parishes. At the time of writing St. Saviour and Trinity have voted not to join the scheme, while St. Ouen, character-istically, have gone their own way with a number of designated 'Scenic Lanes', without the 15 mph speed limit.

This development must be welcomed by all those who are not exclusively car drivers, though dedicated footpaths would obviously be preferred by walkers. At present, Jersey's Green Lanes are not, as a mainlander may imagine, unmetalled tracks, but single carriageway roads, usually flanked by high hedges, in which cars are restricted but not prohibited. Indeed, it it unlikely that they will ever be free of cars as they provide the sole access to certain properties en route.

## GREFFIER

The clerks to the **States** and the **Royal Court** are known as *greffiers*, and each has his/her own responsibilities. The registration of titles to property known as *contrats* is the responibility of the *Greffier* of the Royal Court – a local land registry was set up in 1602 when Sir Walter Raleigh was Governor of Jersey. Most of the work is now computerised.

## GUIDE BOOKS

Wherever there are tourists there are guide books to direct their readers to local 'objects of interest', as the Victorians described sights worth visiting, and provided those interested a chance to learn something about the history and special character of the locality.

One of the earliest guide books to the Island is entitled *A Picture of Jersey, or Stranger's Companion through that Island*, written by one J. Stead and published in Jersey in 1809. A steady stream of publications followed, by a range of authors, most with some original material, but many with material which was shamelessly plagiarised from existing books. Indeed, on reading some of these guide books, you quite often experience a powerful feeling of *deja vu* when you read a sentence, or a paragraph or, indeed, several consecutive pages which you've already encountered, word for word, in an earlier book.

Another point is that individual guide books often tell you as much, if not more, about the author than about Jersey, in particular, whether his attitude is open-minded and genuinely curious or prejudiced and patronising, and we shall sample a range of attitudes in the passages quoted below. First Mr. Stead, one of the pioneers of the Jersey guide book; here he is describing, in typically florid style, his arrival at St. Helier, when Fort Regent was under construction:

> 'An immense Bay, sheltered from every wind but the S.W. the Water scarcely rippled by the Gale, majestic Rocks intersected by deep vallies rejoicing in the Fruitfulness surrounding their vine-covered Cottages; and on the Right, the imposing Mountain called the Mont de la Ville, animated by the numerous Workmen employed in completing its Fortifications.'

The demands of tourism are as much a source of controversy today as they ever were. The least intrusive kind of tourism depends upon the attitude and expectations of tourists. It is the spirit of adventure which marks out the true traveller. Others are disappointed if they do not find everything arranged to suit their own convenience and do not wish to adapt to local custom – one wonders why such people ever leave home. Here is Octavius Rooke, in 1862, with a suggestion as to how Jersey might improve its facilities for the benefit of tourists:

> 'It is a matter of surprise that the inhabitants do not more study their own interests, by subscribing with greater liberality to so popular an amusement as boat-racing; nowhere in the U.K. can there be a more favourable course for the public to see without the trouble of embarking, and doubtless the extra attraction of such amusements would amply repay the tradesmen, etc. who might subscribe to them, by bringing more visitors to pass the summer in the island.'

And here is Mr. Rooke complaining about the lack of guide posts at road junctions:

'On coming to the junction of roads, we keep straight on. And here I may remark that there is, to the best of my belief, not one guide-post in the island: it is perfectly shameful that the people, who profit by the visits of strangers to the island, do not pay a little more attention to their comfort.'

But the guide book writers were, thankfully, not all like Octavius Rooke. Many were happy to explore and delighted in the differentness of Jersey:

'An experienced traveller will always be content to take a thing as he finds it. And if he comes to Jersey with a disposition to be pleased, he can hardly be disappointed.'

The nineteenth century guide books nearly always recommend a number of tours through the Island, by which tourists might see everything deemed worthwhile. Star attractions included the Troglodyte Caves in a disused clay pit in St. Saviour where so called caves were adorned with thousands of shells and an artificial lake was crossed by a miniature paddle boat; the tropical gardens at La Claire, Rozel; the maze, which was a copy of the one at Hampton Court Palace, at the Old Pontac Hotel at St. Clement and, last but most importantly, the Prince's Tower at La Hougue Bie. The archaeological significance of Hougue Bie lay unrecognised until the dig of 1924. It had previously been the site of a hotel, skittle alley and a gazebo, known as the Prince's Tower, which was erected atop the old chapel which today surmounts the great mound. Tourists flocked to this most celebrated spot to admire the view.

Henry Inglis was more than a tourist; he lived in Jersey for two years, edited a newspaper and wrote his own two-volume guide to the Channel Islands. Here he is on the Prince's Tower:

'I have never failed to be delighted with the view from this spot, which is not only interesting, as at once laying open the whole character and extent of the island, but as being in itself, inexpressibly beautiful. Jersey appears like an extensive pleasure ground, – one immense park, thickly studded with trees; beautifully undulating, and dotted with cottages ... the whole island is seen spread out like a map at your feet.'

*Prince's Tower, from an early engraving.*

The early tourists were expected to make their own arrangements in hiring horses and carriages, or perhaps to embark on a pedestrian tour, and to arrange for places to stay en route. At a later date came the excursion car, i.e. organised tour, then the motor coach tour and finally the self-drive hire car.

Early tourists had a romantic attraction to nature and loved to be awed by anything wild and untamed. In his guide book of 1809, J. Stead, blissfully ignorant of the onward march of La Moye Golf Club, has this to say about the sand dunes of Quennevais (which he anglicises to 'Canveys'):

'The Country in one Part wears an appearance of Sterility that would induce a Stranger to believe he was suddenly transported into the Deserts of Arabia; the Road leading through what are called the Canveys, a Tract of many Acres of Land, which in the year 1495, is said to have been equally fruitful with the adjacent Country; in that Year, a mighty Whirlwind covered it with immense Hills of Sand that now render it frightful with Barrenness. The Hills in some Places are so frequent and lofty, and their Shapes so much alike that without an experienced Guide a Person might perish amidst their dreary Solitude ... The Hurricane which produced this Devastation must have been dreadful, as they are raised full one hundred Feet above the Elevation of the Sea and extend more than a Mile from the Shore.'

For the majority of today's tourists it is surely the natural beauties of Jersey which remain her major attractions.

# H

## HUGO, Victor

The great French writer, now perhaps best known for his book *Les Miserables* on which the successful musical of the same name is based, is also responsible for the well known description of the Channel Islands as, 'Morceaux de France tombes à la mer et ramasses par l'Angleterre', i.e. 'pieces of France fallen into the sea and gathered up by England.'

Regarded as a dangerous radical in his native land, Hugo arrived in Jersey in 1852 as one of the so called 'Proscrits'; his wife described her new home as follows:

> 'The country is superb, and all articles of food are abundant, easily obtained and a little cheaper than in Paris. The land is pre-eminently that of freedom. Policemen are unknown. Passports are papers of which the meaning is not understood. Everybody comes and goes as suits his particular fancy ... winter is coming soon, and here people dance a great deal, stupidly, but they still dance.'

Hugo's sojourn in Jersey between 1852 and 1855 is recorded in a plaque set into the rock (known as *Le Rocher des Proscrits*) at the Dicq. His home in Jersey was a house backing on to the nearby beach, part of Marine Terrace. This site was later occupied by the Victor Hugo Hotel, which, during the Occupation, was the official brothel for German soldiers. The site is now redeveloped as a large block of apartments quite out of scale with the location.

Hugo was tolerated by his Jersey hosts until his newspaper, *L'Homme*, in 1855 attacked Queen Victoria, though he himself was not responsible. Loyal Jersey folk attacked his publishing office and demanded the paper be suppressed. Hugo protested that the right to free speech be upheld but he and some other *proscrits* were expelled. Some, indeed, settled in England but Hugo and his family moved to Guernsey where he wrote *Les Miserables* and *Toilers of the Sea*, which latter book rather caricatured the Guernsey folk's way of life.

## HUGUENOTS

The protracted struggle in France between the Roman Catholic Church and the Protestants led to successive waves of persecution of the Protestant Huguenots. They first arrived in Jersey during the 1530s; another influx followed in 1685 when Louis XIV unleashed persecution on the Protestants. Thousands of Huguenots were expelled; large numbers arrived in Jersey and some stayed, thereby strengthening Jersey's French-speaking community and its Protestant leanings. De Faye is one well known Jersey family of Huguenot descent.

## HYDRANGEA

Jersey is often described as an 'Island of Flowers'. Many species are grown for the market, most notably carnations, which are raised under glass. Of all the flowers which may be seen in Jersey throughout the year, perhaps the most memorable is the hydrangea – a large, bushy, big-leaved plant with an abundance of showy flowers. As one observer has noted: 'The hydrangea is not more remarkable for the large size it attains and the abundance of its blossom than for the singular admixture of pink and blue flowers it produces.' Jersey hydrangeas are indeed remarkable. They appear to grow wild and bloom over a long period. And the dried-out flower heads are attractive in their own right.

# I

## IMMIGRATION

Jersey has long carried on a flourishing sea-borne trade with France, Britain and much further afield, notably Newfoundland, which led to an inevitable exchange of people as well as goods. And, because Jersey is close to France yet subject to the British Crown, it has long been a place of refuge, especially for dissident Frenchmen – the Protestant **Huguenots** in particular – but also French Royalists and Catholic clergy at the time of the Revolution.

Very large numbers arrived from the British mainland when the Napoleonic Wars were concluded in 1815, chiefly ex-Arrny and Navy officers, pensioned off on half-pay, who found the living cheaper in tax-free Jersey. And men were needed to work on great public works, like St. Helier's new harbour and St. Catherine's Breakwater, which were constructed after the end of hostilities; many of these came from Ireland. Numbers of French subjects arrived, also, and came to dominate the hotel industry. Improved transport facilities, notably the advent of the steam packet, encouraged tourists and some of these liked what they saw sufficiently to swell the ranks of the **residents**.

The English influx ensued throughout the nineteenth century and, indeed, continues to this day. Many seasonal workers in the agricultural industry, chiefly from Brittany, began to arrive towards the end of the 1800s, though these were replaced by Portuguese nationals, largely from the island of Madeira, from the 1960s onwards.

As well as the Portuguese, a large number of whom work in the hotel and catering industry, there are communities of Spaniards, Italians, Greeks, Chinese, Indians and many others in the Island today. Like the mainland, this diverse immigrant admixture makes life more interesting, not least in the variety of cuisine available in local restaurants. On the other hand, the distinctiveness of Jersey's indigenous population inevitably becomes diluted, as is the case in almost every characteristic region of England.

It seems remarkable that so much of the Jersey character, not to mention the native Jersey Norman-French tongue, has survived. No doubt we have the local farming families and the Jersey law of inheritance to thank for that. The old landed families have often preferred to intermarry, thereby maintaining the 'purity' of the stock, rather like the Jersey cow. But with the increasing pressure to which Island agriculture is now subjected, one wonders how much longer this will be the case.

The visitor cannot help but notice, amongst the 'locals' he or she encounters – the shop assistants, bar staff, bus drivers and cabbies – an extraordinary diversity of British regional accents. Scots first and foremost, followed by Irish from both sides of the border, Geordie, Scouse, the flat vowels of Yorkshire and the fruitier ones of Lancashire, the Cockney or 'Estuary English' of the south-east and almost everything in between.

**Population** figures since the last war have increased steadily, largely through immigration, and recently there have been determined efforts to stem the tide.

## INHERITANCE
According to current Jersey law a testator may devise his real estate freely as he wishes, save that the dower rights of a succeeding widow survive. In recent times this right takes the form of the life enjoyment of the matrimonial home and certain other rights to movable effects and other rights including a sum

of money. The law details these provisions known as 'Wills and Succession (Jersey Law) 1993.'

In former times, Jersey law dictated that real estate was not left in accordance with the whim of the testator. A wife had an automatic life interest in one-third of her husband's estate on the day of their marriage and in that which he might inherit during his lifetime. The remaining two-thirds was divided among the children. The eldest son was entitled to a number of privileges, which accounts for the tradition among younger sons to go to sea or emigrate. The residue was divided in the proportion of two-thirds to the sons (including the eldest son) and one-third to the daughters, but that no daughter shall receive a larger share than a son.

Farms were thus divided and sub-divided among the children, though it was usually the case that the eldest son bought out the interests of his siblings in order to guarantee the viability of his smallholding. In this way the continued prosperity of the owner-farmers was maintained and this, in turn, did much to protect a traditional way of life, methods of agriculture and the characteristic appearance of the countryside.

# J

## JERRIAIS

The most significant point about the native Jersey tongue, Jèrriais, or Jersey Norman-French, is that it is traditionally a spoken language, not a written one. Here is a quote from Stead, who wrote one of the very first guide books to Jersey, published in 1809:

'The language of the Natives is the old French of Normandy: not so corrupt as it is obsolete and antiquated French. It is almost daily falling into Disuse and Discredit, and doubtless, in a few years hence, English will be the only prevailing language amongst the People.'

Another contemporary noted, in 1822:

'Although the English language is spoken by all ranks of people, yet the very old Norman French is that of the lower orders, and of which they are so tenacious, that they are unwilling to speak English, although they know it. Good French however is taught in the island, by the French professors.'

What these observations indicate is that many Jersey folk were trilingual – in English, 'Good French' and Jersey-French. Whilst 'Good French' was tolerated, even respected, English observers seemed to have nothing but contempt for the local tongue and predicted its imminent demise with relish.

Traditionally, English was the everyday language of commerce, 'Good French' was reserved for church and chapel, the Royal Court, the States and some newspapers, whilst Jersey-French was the spoken language of the country folk. Indeed, it was so indigenous that, even today, there are significant differences in vocabulary and usage between the Jèrriais spoken in the west of the Island as compared to that in the east.

No doubt it is a privilege to speak Jèrriais and that this 'secret' language came in very useful in dealing with the sometimes predatory English, as well as with the German occupiers during World War II. Guernsey French has distinct differences to Jersey French but the native language of Sark is reckoned to be the closest to that spoken in Normandy.

There is a considerable revival of interest in Jèrriais today. Many people are conversant in it, even some not of the Island. Nevertheless, English is generally more dominant than ever – in the religious, legal and political as well as social life of the Island – a position which it is difficult to see being shifted.

Let us add the voice of David Ansted, a more thoughtful and sympathetic observer than many of his contemporaries, at the close of the nineteenth century:

'From many points of view it would be regrettable should this venerable dialect, preserved intact through eight long centuries and still heard almost in its pristine purity, and with which many an ancient tradition is inextricably linked, be suffered to disappear.'

When one hears Jèrriais being spoken, one immediately recognises the source of the distinctive Jersey accent. Some French names are today sometimes pronounced in a French fashion and sometimes Anglicised, but when Jèrriais is being spoken, the names will surely be pronounced *à la Français*.

# JERSEY

## 1. Name

The name 'Jersey' first appeared in a charter of 1025, following the arrival of the Normans, though the initial 'J' was often replaced with a 'G'. The second syllable 'ey' is Norse for island, as in Guernsey, Alderney, Sheppey, Orkney, etc. The first syllable may refer to a personal name.

Jersey has lent its name to the U.S. state of New Jersey, founded in 1664, and to Jerseyville and Jersey County in Illinois. The word 'Jersey' has entered the English language to refer to the knitted fabric and garment of which Jersey had a huge output during the heyday of the local knitting industry.

The Jersey lily, *amaryllis belladonna*, is less famous, but perhaps more so as the epithet by which Lillie Langtry became widely known. The Jersey Tiger Moth is a spectacularly coloured variety found in the Island; the 'Jerseyman' was the name given to the red-legged partridge, once commonplace but now extinct – the last specimen was shot at Plémont in 1876.

## 2. Shape

Jersey is an indented rectangle. The western corners and north coast are composed of the most resistant rocks to withstand the assault of the Atlantic. Looking at the outline of the Island, one has a sense of the Island advancing westwards, out of the clutches of the Bay of Mont St. Michel, and trailing in its wake a great litter of low scattered rocks to the south-east. One writer has said of the Island that it is 'shaped like a tiger with its head facing west'. Guernsey, on the other hand, with its headlands facing south and east, but trailing low rocks to the west, looks as though it feels it has strayed too far out into the ocean and is attempting to return.

**JERSEY-FRENCH** *see* **JERRIAIS**

## JERSEY SOCIETY IN LONDON

Celebrated its centenary in 1996, so constitutes one of the very few remaining 'provincial' societies in London which surely attests to the Jerseyman's enduring love of his homeland. Its homesick founder was Arthur Balleine (1864-1943).

For many years the organisation was restricted to men largely working in the professions, who met together to attend learned lectures as well as an annual dinner – traditionally held on the anniversary of the Duke of Normandy's invasion of England. The Society's membership today is made up of a wide cross section of folk who still, for the most, have Jersey roots. They gather regularly for meetings which are addressed by speakers on subjects of Jersey interest and publish an excellent journal, *The Bulletin* (not to be confused with the *Annual Bulletin* of La Société Jersiaise). A dinner was held in 1996 to mark the centenary. *Jersey Society in London, Hon. Secretary, 66 Townfield, Rickmansworth, WD3 2DD.*

## JURAT

There are twelve jurats, elected to office by an electoral college, who act as lay assessors in matters of fact and as advisors to the Bailiff or whoever sits as Judge in civil and criminal cases. It is deemed a great honour to be so elected. The office dates back to shortly after 1204. Jurats sit with the Bailiff when cases are heard before the Royal Court.

They do not retain as much power as they did in former times, but still occupy an important place in the Island's system of **law** and **government**. Retirement age is 72 years.

# L

## LANGTRY, Lillie
Jersey's most famous (some would say infamous) daughter, she was born Lillie Le Breton in 1853. Lillie became a renowned actress, fêted by Royalty and the literati, including Oscar Wilde. She returned to Jersey in 1900 to open the Opera House. Lillie – 'The Jersey lily' – possessed considerable business acumen and amassed a fortune; she wrote her life story and died in Monaco, where she spent the last decade of her life; in 1929 her body was brought back to Jersey and lies buried at St. Saviour's Church.

## LAVOIR
More properly termed a *douet à lavoir*, this is a communal washing place, to be found in most Island parishes. A stream was dammed to form a pool and the women would gather to wash their clothes and, no doubt, to exchange news. Many *lavoirs* are impressive structures hewn from the native granite.

## LAW
The roots of Jersey's system of law reach back to the days of the Norman Empire, before 1204, when the Channel Islands sided with England against France, and has adapted itself to changing circumstances ever since. Indeed, a good deal has been done in recent years to simplify and modernise the old legal system, particularly regarding tenure, conveyance of property and **inheritance**, but not necessarily based on English practice.

Although Jersey enjoys considerable autonomy in matters of

law, there has always been a firm link with Britain in that Acts of the States must receive the Royal Ascent by Order in the Privy Council before they are enacted.

Law officers, including the Attorney-General and Solicitor General, are Crown appointments; they act on behalf of the Crown and the States and are legal advisers to the States.
*see also* GOVERNMENT, JURAT.

## LIEUTENANT-GOVERNOR (formerly Governor)
The Lieutenant-Governor of Jersey is appointed by the British Crown for a term of five years and is the Sovereign's representative in the Island. In his absence, the **Bailiff** assumes his role at official functions. Since 1923, the Lieutenant-Governor has resided at Government House in St. Saviour. Before that (and during the time of the Battle of Jersey in 1781) the Lieutenant-Governor lived at a residence in Grosvenor Street which was knocked down a few years after the German Occupation. Previously some Governors lived at Elizabeth Castle.

## The LOTTERY
The Jersey lottery is held weekly and the £1 tickets are sold through registered agents – shops and booths – and a top prize of £45,000 is currently offered. Anyone may purchase a ticket and in the days before the UK National Lottery was introduced in 1994, a flutter on the Jersey Lottery was an attraction for many visitors to the Island.

There is something of a tradition of lotteries in Jersey, notwithstanding the ethos you would expect of its predominantly Methodist population. Indeed, when General Sir George Don was Governor at the beginning of the nineteenth century, he introduced a lottery to help raise money to meet the cost of his road-building programme. Even before that, the States began a lottery in 1788 to raise money for the defence of the Island against the French.

# M

## MARRIAGE STONE

The marriage stone is a rather appealing custom which, however, probably does not date back further than the seventeenth century. The lintel over the front door of a dwelling is carved with the initials (usually three letters) of the marriage partners; sometimes they are joined by a pair of interlocking hearts.

## MARTELLO TOWER

The defensive towers dotted around Jersey's coastline are generally referred to as Martello towers, though this appellation is more accurately applied only to the type of tower constructed after 1794. The first round towers were built on the recommendation of Governor Henry Seymour Conway in 1778. In the following year he claimed that four had been completed, Grève de Lecq being the oldest survivor.

The Battle of Jersey in 1781 lent added urgency to the building programme and several towers, including the offshore Seymour Tower (with its unique square plan), were erected along the low-lying and vulnerable south-east coast. These original Jersey towers are circular in plan – about 35 feet across at the base, tapering to 29 feet at the summit. The lower level acted as a store for weapons and supplies whilst the upper level provided accommodation for the troops – one officer and ten men. Above them was the gun platform where, most often, one heavy cannon was fixed to a rotating platform. Some 22 of these Jersey round towers were erected, all before 1800.

The name 'Martello' is derived from a tower in Point Mortella in Corsica which was found to be effective against the British and was adopted in 1794 – a particular design of tower which also forms the basis of the many to be found along the Kent coast. Kempt Tower in St. Ouen's Bay is a good example, though it was not built until 1834; it is certainly worthy of a visit in its own right and not only because it houses an exhibition on the Les Mielles conservation area.

Eight true Martello towers were erected in Jersey, all in the first half of the nineteenth century. The last is Victoria Tower on the hill-top above Gorey. It is rather small, moated and affords panoramic views; it is now used as an astronomical observatory. Today, 24 towers out of the 31 built are extant, those missing having been destroyed by the action of the sea or the Germans. La Rocco Tower, built on rocks in St. Ouen's Bay, perhaps the most memorable of all, has been reconstructed after being used for target practice during the Occupation.

*Martello Tower as represented in a guide book published in 1856; it must represent the one at Grève de Lecq, with the rather knobbly outline of Sark on the horizon.*

## MARY ANN

This was a favourite girl's name in nineteenth century Jersey and several Jersey sailing ships bore the same name. Today, Mary Ann is best known as Jersey's own brew, and is made by the Ann Street Brewery, a concern which dates back to at least 1871. The Brewery's current slogan is, 'Mary Ann – the Beers that made Jersey famous' when it would probably be truer to declare: 'Jersey – the Island that made Mary Ann beers famous.' There is also a longstanding slogan, 'Ask for Mary Ann.' It is immortalised in neon above the Great Western Hotel at the Weighbridge – another phrase evocative of past times!

In 1871 there were no less than eleven small breweries in Jersey, In recent times, Ann Street's only competitor was Randall's, but this company ceased brewing in 1993. Real ale fanciers have long been unimpressed with the mainly fizzy, refrigerated stuff which today goes under the name of Mary Ann (though its lagers are greatly admired), so it was indeed a welcome development when the Tipsy Toad brewery hopped on to the scene in 1992, with its brewery/pub at The Star in St. Peter's, and, since 1995, a second brewery/pub at The Town House in New Street, St. Helier. The Tipsy Toad produces a range of tasty ales.

## MINQUIERS

The Minquiers (generally pronounced 'Minkies'), is a reef of rocks and small islands situated south of St. Helier, slightly nearer Jersey than France, administered by the Parish of Grouville. France has periodically laid claim to the area and, like the **Ecréhous** to the north, the case was decided in Jersey's favour at the International Court in 1953. The reef covers an area which is actually greater than Jersey, though much of it submerged at high tide.

Quantities of granite have been quarried in the Minquiers and brought to Jersey and it was once the home of a flourishing oyster industry controlled by fisherfolk from Gorey. Maîtresse Ile has a few buildings, including a Jersey Customs House, but no

— ASK FOR —

**MARY ANN**

Jersey's Famous
ALES
AND
STOUT

*Something to write home about*

BREWED AND BOTTLED ONLY BY

# ANN STREET BREWERY
## COMPANY, LIMITED

permanent population. As the most southerly point in the British Isles, the Minquiers formed the starting point of the television series 'Island Race' featuring Sandi Toskvig and John McCarthy, first broadcast in 1995.

## MONEY

You sense that there must be plenty of it in Jersey, with St. Helier bursting at the seams with banks, financial institutions and shops stuffed with jewellery. There is traditionally a high level of prosperity, even without this evidence, so noticeable in the late twentieth century. Fertile soil, a favourable climate and the hard work and thriftiness of the native population, laid the basis of the Island's wealth. And sea-borne trade, including privateering and smuggling, certainly made a large contribution. Jersey cannot be described as other than a comparatively wealthy community. Indeed, in 1996 it was reported that bank deposits in Jersey stood in excess of £90.4 billion, the highest level ever, more than £1,000,000 for every man, woman and child in the Island, though the bulk of this huge amount is owned by overseas investors.

One of the first things the visitor from the mainland notices is the money in his pocket – it is similar but different to English money. The coins may be the same shape and size but the designs are distinctive, though all carry the Sovereign's head. The pound coin is absent and is replaced by a friendly, if often tatty, green note (though this may not be the case for much longer).

It was not until the nineteenth century that Jersey had its own coinage – until then the recognised standard of money was the *livres tournais*, the coinage minted in Tours, but tokens were often minted locally to compensate for a shortage of the official coinage. There was a change from French to English coinage in 1834 when a pound sterling was equated with 26 *livres tournois*. In 1841, Jersey began issuing its own copper and bronze coins on which the Sovereign's head appears. Guernsey's currency does not carry the Sovereign's head and, for this reason, appears much more 'foreign' than Jersey's. You frequently handle Guernsey currency in Jersey, as well as Scottish banknotes. Indeed, with the lack of colour coordination between the various bank notes in circulation, great care must be exercised by the unsuspecting visitor.

## MURATTI

The Muratti is the highlight of the soccer season in the Channel Islands; the annual contest between Jersey and Guernsey takes place in each island in alternate years. The trophy – the Muratti Vase – was originally donated in 1905 as a publicity stunt by the manufacturers of Muratti Cigarettes, now long forgotten.

The record of results shows that, since its inception, the cup has been shared almost equally between Jersey and Guernsey, with Guernsey dominant before the Occupation years, and Jersey since. Little Alderney has only won once – in 1921, when they beat Guernsey 1 - 0 at Westmount, Jersey.

The name 'Muratti' has been borrowed to denote any inter-island competition, so that the word has entered the language and taken on a life of its own.

# N

## NATIONAL TRUST FOR JERSEY
This organisation was founded in 1936 in the cause of the acquisition, maintenance and preservation of places of historic interest and natural beauty. The Jersey Trust is, perhaps, stronger in its ownership of parcels of land than country houses, with which its mainland counterpart is most often associated. You often encounter, as you travel around the Island, unobtrusive notices indicating a piece of land as National Trust property, usually shown as 'Le Don xxx', the xxx denoting the origin of the gift.

## The NORMANS
Jersey was converted to **Christianity** well before the arrival of the Normans, in the days when Jersey was closely connected to the Celtic strongholds of Brittany, Cornwall and Ireland. Nevertheless, the Channel Islands, or Les Iles Anglo-Normandes, were much more thoroughly 'Normanised' than the mainland, with its Celtic and Saxon roots, though how much survives of the pre-Norman parochial basis of law and government is open to question.

Duke William I of Normandy incorporated the Channel Islands into the Duchy in about 933, where they remained for almost three centuries. The Normans introduced the feudal system and carved up Jersey into a number of fiefs which were lorded over by newly arrived Norman families. It is from these original settlers that many of Jersey's old families are descended. The author's family name, Le Dain, probably means 'The Dane', which would appear to be indisputably of Norman origin, though it is doubtful that the first Le Dain arrived in Jersey before about 1500.

With the retreat of the Norman Empire, which at its height stretched from Scandinavia to the Eastern Mediterranean, came the question of Jersey's future status – should it remain loyal to the Norman King of England, or ally itself with France, to which it was so closely tied? It is likely that this was a highly political decision, that the local overlords, fearing for their wealth and influence, chose to remain on the side from which they were more likely to wrest independence from their powerful neighbours on the French mainland. At the same time they were able to extract many favours from King John, in return for their loyalty to the British Crown, privileges which Jersey enjoys to this day.

# O

## ORMER

A local shellfish. The word is a contraction of *oreille de mer*, or 'ear of the sea' – a picturesque and not inaccurate description of the shell's appearance. It clings to rocks which may be exposed at particularly low tides, known as ormering tides. The Channel Islands mark the northern limit of the ormer's habitat.

The ormer is a highly regarded delicacy and afficionados will expend much time and energy searching them out. They are not easily found and, as a result, demand a high price on the market. In recent years there have been efforts to farm ormers, though this has met with mixed success.

The rule is that one may only gather ormers during months which have an 'R' in them, i.e. September to April; May to August are forbidden. Ormers eaten out of season have been known to have drastic effects – grotesquely swollen lips being one effect. This may be put down to food poisoning from the ormers – and just retribution for collecting them at a forbidden time!

To prepare ormers for the table you first remove the soft contents from the shell, scrub, beat and rub with flour. Fry in butter until brown, then stew or casserole with a lump of pork or bacon and seasoning and leave to simmer for several hours until tender.  The shells, whose iridescent interior resembles mother of pearl, were at one time sent to Birmingham to be worked into *papier maché* products.

# **P**

## PARISH

Jersey is divided into twelve parishes, in alphabetical order they are as follows: Grouville, St. Brelade, St. Clement, St. Helier, St. John, St. Lawrence, St. Martin, St. Mary, St. Ouen, St. Peter, St. Saviour and Trinity. St. Ouen, which covers much of the comparatively wild landscape of the west and north west, is the largest in area and, with the exception of neighbouring St. Mary, the most sparsely populated. At the other extreme, St. Clement has less than a third the area of St. Ouen but is much more densely populated, though only around half that of St. Helier. All parishes border the sea, though St. Saviour only manages it by a whisker.

The parochial map of Jersey is reckoned to date back more than a millenium and the five central parishes – St. John, St. Lawrence, St. Mary, St. Peter and St. Saviour – date from around 475, though all twelve existed when the Normans arrived in 933AD. Fragments of pre-Norman building may be traced in some of the parish churches, notably St. Lawrence.

The parish assemblies may have evolved before the coming of the **Normans** – the men of the parish meeting to attend to parish business under their elected **Constable** who, with his elected **Centeniers** and **Vingteniers**, formed the honorary **police**, organised on a Parish basis. Officers of the Parish also include the Procureurs de bien Public (Public Trustees), Churchwardens, Constable's Officers and the Almoner, with a distinction between the civil parish and the eccesiastical parish (Rector,

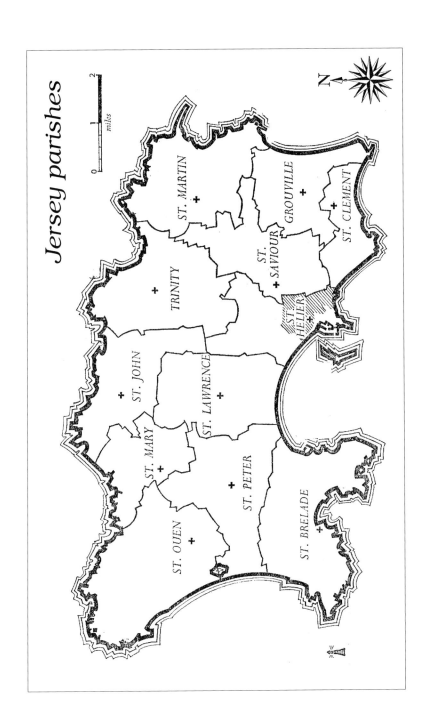

*Jersey parishes*

Churchwardens and Almoner). All are elected by the Parish Assembly and are unpaid. The only exception is the Rector, appointed by the Crown. Funds to run the parish are raised by rates and parish responsibilities include social welfare, repairs to minor roads, street lighting, refuse collection, local policing and issuing of licences for drivers, dogs and firearms, as well as the upkeep of the parish church and rectory.

When the conquering Duke of Normandy carved up the Island into fiefs under the ownership of the **Seigneurs**, it is likely that the parish assemblies and their elected representatives and officials exerted a modifying influence on the powers of their new overlords. The parish organisation endures to this day and has always been a power to reckon with. In the nineteenth century it constituted a countervailing influence to the ascendency of the town of St. Helier, the influx of English residents and the creeping Anglicisation of the Island.

## PATERNOSTERS

A rocky reef directly north of Grève de Lecq on the north coast, otherwise known as Pierres de Lecq. In the sixteenth century, when Helier de Carteret of Jersey was colonising Sark, one of his ships came to grief on these rocks and several children were drowned. It was said that, whenever a storm arose, their cries were heard. The rocks were subsequently held in some  awe and sailors became accustomed to reciting the Lord's Prayer (*Pater Noster* = Our Father) when they passed them.

## PERQUAGE

The old French word for the sanctuary paths which formerly led from Jersey's parish churches to the sea. Until the Reformation, these churches possessed, in accordance with Norman law, the *Franchise de l'Eglise*, or right of sanctuary, within their walls. In addition, from each church there was a sanctuary way or *perquage* which led to the sea and could be used as a means of escape from the island. The parish rector usually accompanied the wrongdoer to the waiting boat where he wished him godspeed and a future life of atonement; any deviation from the path would risk arrest by the parish **constable**.

The right of sanctuary was abolished at the Reformation when the *perquages* became Crown property and then, in 1663, were granted by King Charles II to the de Carterets in recognition of the family's loyalty to him during the Civil War. Later still the *perquages* were sold off piecemeal and incorporated into private property. The only surviving fragment, apart from the flight of steps which lead from St. Brelade's church to the beach, is the stretch of pleasant path between Goose Green and St. Aubin's Bay which once formed part of the sanctuary path from St. Lawrence Church. It seems a particularly sad loss – there's no doubt that, had they survived, the Jersey *perquages* would today form a footpath network of unique historical significance.

The concept of the sanctuary path must have encouraged the notion that troublesome individuals could be exported; I think it is fair to suggest that such a sentiment lives on in the attitude that asserts, "If you don't like it here, go to a better place!" A problem sent out of the Island is effectively a problem solved.

## PHYSICAL TYPE

Here are some quotes, describing the natives, from early guide books written by Englishmen abroad in the foreign land of Jersey:

'They are mostly short, dark and not especially good-looking.'

'They are not, generally speaking, a handsome people. Of the stature and appearance of the men, a better test cannot be obtained, than the island militia; and certainly, after a review of the 3 or 4,000 that compose this force, one must decide, that the race does not offer many examples of handsome countenances ... constant intermarriage will infallibly lead to a deterioration of the race. An ungenerous diet, will also have its effects: unwearied outdoor labour is the enemy of beauty, and unfavourable to erectness of form: and to this must be added, want of sleep, which I look upon to be a distinguishing characteristic of the country people of Jersey.'

This last, withering account was written in 1840. A hundred years later, Jersey resident R.C.F. Maugham, in his book, *The Island of Jersey Today*, propagates an extraordinary theory that the natives of Jersey are derived from the Jewish diaspora:

'There seems every indication the ancient dwellers on the Normandy and Brittany coasts of France did actually become dominated by one or more of the wandering Hebraic hordes seeking a permanent refuge remote from those Palestinian upheavals that had banished them from the land of their fathers, what could be more probable than that the resulting coast races inhabiting the Cotentin crossed over to the Channel Islands and people them as well?'

His book was first published in 1939; one must conclude that, thankfully, a copy did not find its way into the hands of the Nazi Commandant. Maugham's theory was perhaps prompted by the typical Jerseyman's short and swarthy physical appearance. The amateur anthropologist Maugham continues as follows:

'They are well formed, and often well developed; those leading an active, outdoor existence are strong and muscular, and doubtless able to endure a great amount of manual labour without undue fatigue. I have observed few instances of inclination to steatopygy, which is, perhaps, more observable in the women than the men. On the whole, I fancy, the gluteal muscles, among the country people at any rate, are well developed, and carriage fairly upright.'

The dictionary defines steatopygy as 'excessive development of fat on the buttocks, especially of women.'

In her recent book on the war years, *A Model Occupation*, author Madeleine Bunting writes of incest as commonplace in pre-war times, and that 'over the years the large mental hospital at St. Saviour's housed many of the products of these relationships.' If this assertion is as accurate as much else that her book contains, then it should be taken with a large pinch of salt.

## PLACE NAMES

Almost all Jersey place names outside St. Helier, are of French, or Norman French, origin. One Celtic survival is St. Brelade, whose name is thought to be a corruption of St. Brendan, the Irish missionary.

Many common elements crop up in Jersey place names, as follows:

**carrefour**: crossroads, e.g. Carrefour Selous;
**clos**: a field, e.g. many examples in recent housing schemes;
**douet**: stream, e.g. Faldouet: swiftly flowing stream;
**grève**: beach, e.g. Grève de Lecq, Grève d'Azette;
**hougue**: prehistoric burial ground, e.g. La Hougue Bie, Le Hocq;
**marais**: marsh, e.g. Samares (= 'salt marsh');
**mielle**: sand dune, e.g. Les Mielles;
**moie**: a mass of stones, e.g. La Moye;
**pouquelaye**: prehistoric burial ground marked by stones.

There were once some 50 such sites in the Island, many of which survive.

All names ending in the letter Q, such as The Dicq, L'Etacq, are on the coast and stem from Scandinavian words.

The above represents but a drop in the ocean of Jersey place names. Many names may be ascribed to family and individual association; many are corrupted by generations of usage so that what seems an obvious origin may not be so. A serious student of Jersey place names should seek out the scholarly and comprehensive study *Jersey Place Names*, published by Société Jersiase.

## Honorary POLICE

An ancient and enduring institution based on the parish which finds its origin in pre-Norman times. The **Parish** assembly, consisting of the parish officials and the principals of the parish (i.e. all ratepayers assessed above a certain figure) is headed by the **Constable**. He is elected by the parishioners, though elections are rarely contested, for a term of three years. The Parish officers include two **Centeniers** and a number of **Vingteniers**, also elected. It is the Constable, assisted by his centeniers and vingteniers, which form Jersey's honorary police. The Attorney General, a Crown appointment, is head of the honorary police.

Until 1952 the paid police force was only operative in St. Helier; today the professional police are active throughout the Island but, outside St. Helier, only with the consent of the respective parish Constable. In theory, only the Constable and his centeniers have the power to arrest, where other members of the honorary police and the paid police may levy a fine on the spot; other cases are brought to the Constable who has the power to settle minor matters himself or to decide whether they shall go before the police court. Each case taken to the police court is in the charge of a centenier who presents it on behalf of the Constable of the parish.

The honorary police system has served Jersey well for a millenium or more though it is becoming increasingly difficult to find people to serve in a voluntary capacity. Interest in the system has been shown in recent years by the UK Government, though one cannot escape the conclusion that its main attraction is the possibility of saving money on law enforcement by employing volunteers, rather than any consideration of effectiveness.

## POPULATION

Population census figures and estimates of population before the census began reveal that Jersey was always a relatively densely populated island. Not surprisingly, perhaps, when one bears in mind the advantages of soil and climate and the surrounding seas which Jersey enjoys. Latterly, of course, especially since the Napoleonic Wars, Jersey has been a magnet for tax-evading Brits and a range of people, especially the young, seeking job opportunities and a place in the sun.

The recent boom in the finance industry has led to a population explosion, with consequent pressure on land and the Island's infrastructure. Strict immigration and housing controls have made an impact but Jersey's continued prosperity, relative to the mainland, cannot be ignored. Jersey's population has grown significantly faster than natural growth, particularly in the 1960s and 1980s when around 10,000 were added each decade; the population figure was 84,000 at the 1991 census. A severe disruption of the Island's population occurred in 1940 when some 10,000 out of a total of 51,000 people chose to leave, though most returned to Jersey during the years following Liberation.

On the other hand, Jersey's laws of **inheritance**, particularly regarding real estate, have resulted in a great diaspora of Jersey folk which has been a fact of Island life for centuries.
*see also* IMMIGRATION

## POST

Jersey's postal services were part of the British Post Office until 1969 when Jersey Postal Administration began issuing its own stamps. Since then, a dazzling variety of definitive and commemorative stamps has been issued and philately in Jersey has developed into big business, as it has in many other small nations. It seems that almost any event or anniversary, no matter how trivial, is these days worthy of a special issue.

Actually, Jersey has genuine reason to be celebrated in the annals of postal history – in 1852 the first of four street letter boxes in the British Isles was installed in Jersey – an original octagonal specimen may be seen today outside the main Post Office in the Central Market. Anthony Trollope, better known as a great and prolific novelist of Victorian England, was Post Office Surveyor at the time. But a Post Office had been established in Jersey in 1794 when a sailing packet plied between Jersey and Weymouth. The first Postmaster was Captain Charles Le Geyt and the first Jersey postie was Mary Godfray, who was appointed in 1798 and continued unaided until 1830!

Jersey issued its own postage stamps during the Occupation – they were designed by Edmund **Blampied** and printed in Paris, and are a far cry but much more interesting and noteworthy than the never-ending flow of gaudy stickers which confront us today.

## POTATO

Its cow may be Jersey's most famous export but the Jersey potato must run a close second. The noble potato has been cultivated as a field crop since the late eighteenth century and exported since the early nineteenth.

Begun around 1880, the new potato industry, based on the Jersey Royal (introduced by Hugh De La Haye and more properly known as the Jersey Royal Fluke) attracted an annual influx of seasonal farm workers, until the 1960s from Brittany, but latterly from Madeira and Portugal. Here is a report from the last century:

'Potatoes are extensively grown in all the principal Channel Islands for the London market, and the quantity sent in the early part of the season is almost incredible. Early potatoes are grown under very favourable circumstances in Jersey and Guernsey, and are ready for the table nearly three weeks in advance of those grown in Cornwall.'

Jersey's potatoes remain the mainstay of the Island's farming industry. Much of Jersey's agricultural land is given over to potato growing, at least in the first half of the year, and annual production is often huge, though the success of the harvest always depends upon climatic conditions here and on the mainland.

A recent innovation, not generally welcomed by non-farmers, is the plastic sheeting which is stretched over the tops of the young shoots to protect them against frost and encourage early growth. The early potato may benefit from this device but the appearance of the countryside certainly does not. It is surprising that enterprising farmers do not rent out their plastic-sheeted côtils as ski-slopes.

# R

## RAILWAYS

Railway mania or, as today's progressive minds would describe it, environment-friendly public transport, made itself felt in Jersey in 1870 when the line from St. Helier to St. Aubin was opened. The present Tourism head office, a handsome edifice, once comprised the St. Helier terminus and there were three stations and several halts en route to St. Aubin where the station and former Railway Hotel now serves as the parish hall of St. Brelade. The line was eventually extended to serve La Moye Quarries in 1884 and reached Corbière in 1899. Traffic reached a peak in the mid-1920s but then declined in the face of competition from buses and private cars. A disastrous fire at St. Aubin's Station in 1936 hastened the closure of the entire line.

The Jersey Eastern Railway ran from Snow Hill and pretty much followed the coast to reach Gorey. It opened in 1873 and closed in 1929. In addition, the Germans laid several miles of new track in order to transport heavy equipment to various parts of the Island.

A number of former railway buildings may be distinguished today though long since converted to other uses – you may even discover old rails planted in the ground in the vicinity of the former terminus at Corbière. The 'Railway Walk', from St. Aubin to Corbière, follows the old track-bed and provides a most pleasant footpath, and now cycleway.

Many people today regret the passing of the railway. The late Mr Pallot, whose Steam Museum in Trinity is one of the most interesting and least celebrated of Jersey's many visitor attractions, continued to fight the case for the restoration of rail transport in Jersey. Indeed, he constructed a circular track, complete with period railway station, locomotives and rolling stock, where the passenger may shunt nostalgically beside fields full of cauliflowers and courgettes in deepest Jersey. It is both bizarre and inspiring.

This may not be an accurate figure, but something like 75% of Jersey's out-of-town population must live within half-a-mile of the former railway lines. Were a train service to be reintroduced and people offered a cheap, rapid, reliable and frequent service to and from town, would this not reduce the Island's enormous volume of motor traffic with all its harmful effects on the environment? But would the powerful car lobby ever allow it to happen?

## RESIDENTS

This term was neatly defined, by one of the early guide book writers, as 'those who reside in a place, without tie or employment.' In today's parlance, residents would be incomers who do not have to work but are here to evade tax and to enjoy the other advantages Jersey has to offer.

The influx of residents began after the ending of the Napoleonic Wars, in 1815, when Army and Navy officers were put on half pay and when mainland taxes were increased to pay for the protracted war. It is ironic how people were patriotic in war but became tax exiles in peace. However, by 1840, the resident population is estimated to have been at least 5,000 strong, and it was this continuing influx which gave rise to the building boom and great expansion of St. Helier throughout the last century. Not only did the residents exert an impact on the physical appearance of Jersey, their presence also led to the gradual Anglicisation of all aspects of life.

Henry Inglis, writing in 1834, makes a pointed comment upon

the contrast between the resident and native population:

'There is one thing very striking, in the aspect of the street population of Jersey, – the extraordinary contrast exhibited between business and idleness. The English residents form a large proportion of the inhabitants; and the English residents have nothing to do. There is therefore, the constant contrast between that portion of the population whose object, and I may even say whose difficulty is, to get quit of time, – and that other portion, the native inhabitants namely, whose object is, to make the most of it. The former, is certainly the more difficult, and the more fatiguing task.'

So how did the English residents pass their time? Here is an account from 1844:

'The indoor amusements of the English residents consist of Dinner-parties, Card-parties, Balls and Concerts. At the Theatre, there are occasional performances by companies of both English and French actors ... but 'the Drama' is at a low and doleful ebb ... Pic-nics are universal in summer, and the Island offers numberless delicious scenes for them, both inland and coastward. Archery-meetings and Cricket-matches are not infrequent; and there are generally Races once a-year. Equestrian field-sports are scarcely possible within so circumscribed an area; ... As for the sea, one may have as much fishing upon it as he pleases, in calm weather; but the coast is too rocky, and therefore too dangerous, for Regattas. As for shooting – no game laws and two or three thousand militia muskets leave hardly anything left to shoot.'

It seems that the residents and the Natives did not much mix; here is a passage from a guide book entitled *Queen of the Isles*, published in 1840:

'The English society of Jersey is quite distinct from the native society. I do not say that they never mingle; but the intercourse is limited and unfrequented ... Many of the English complain of want of hospitality on the part of the native families, of a deficiency in those attentions, which, as strangers, they think they had reason to expect; but I think they complain unjustly ... The chief disadvantage under which Jersey lies is the want of the amusements.'

At least this commentator took the side of the Jersey people in his opinion that the incomers had no right to expect any special attention. Residents usually seemed to believe that they had an absolute right to settle in Jersey and to be waited on by a servile populace. Even a century later, R.C.F. Maugham, in his book *The Island of Jersey Today*, published in 1939, complained of the problems of hiring and retaining servants:

'I have been told, and am still quite willing to believe, that there are good and reliable Jersey servants ... For my own part, and judging from the experiences of a large circle of friends, reliable servants of Jersey birth have become something almost in the nature of a legend. Personally, my acquaintance with Jersey-born maids is confined to one derived from a long procession of young women who, in the early years of our residence, entered our service, remained for a week or two, and retired to make way for others of their casual, highly inefficient sisterhood ... the potato harvest, or the collection and grading of tomatoes, is almost certain to spirit them away for work in the fields.'

Now, of course, with stringent rules regarding immigration, it is impossible for anyone except the super-rich, those individuals deemed 'economically necessary' or the many workers who flock to Jersey to undertake the menial jobs which Jersey people would not consider, to take up residence. With the pressures on an already densely populated Island, it could not, of course, be any other way.

Even in the 1960s it was still possible for a well-heeled English family to move to Jersey, buy a house and settle down. Cecil Chisholm wrote a book entitled *Retire to the Sun*, published in 1961, in which he compares the merits of Spain, France, Portugal, the Canary Islands and Jersey; he comments on Jersey as follows:

'Never have I met keener businessmen. Indeed they may try just a little too hard to wring the last sixpence out of every visitor.'

His conclusion on Jersey is as follows:

'Everything in Jersey tends to be faintly tarty, consciously dolled-up, ever so slightly vulgar. I fancy this is how the resident millionaires and peers rather like it.'

A large proportion of Jersey's population today must descend from successive waves of resident incomers. It is interesting to ask the question, 'When does a resident become a native – how many years or generations does it take? Or must you possess a Norman pedigree, or speak Jersey Norman-French, to count as *un vrai Jèrriais*? And what of the Huguenots, the Bretons and all the other various immigrants from France?

## ROADS

For an island of only 45 square miles, Jersey has a remarkable network of surfaced roads – some 550 miles. And, compared to the mainland, where hard-pressed local authorities have been unable to maintain roads in good repair, those in Jersey are well cared for. This was not always the case; one observer records that, before the Napoleonic Wars:

'The roads are narrow, winding and very intricate, sunk below the level of the land, flanked by enormous mounds, crowded with trees overcanopying them. Carts meeting cannot pass, but must seek the nearest gateway. To this may be attributed the remarkable proficiency of the population in swearing.'

The frustrations of this inefficient system of roads was overcome by General Sir George Don who was Lieutenant Governor of Jersey from 1806 -14. He built a number of new roads, sufficiently wide and straight to allow artillery to gallop and find access to any corner of the Island which was threatened by an enemy. Don's road-building programme was paid for by an increase in the *impôt* (import duty) on spirits, by a newly introduced **lottery** and by grants from the British government as they were considered defence works.

A more poetic observer, David Ansted, has this to say about Jersey's narrow, sunken lanes:

'Very numerous lanes wind about in every direction, apparently without other purpose than to deceive the traveller, and it is safest to conclude that they do not lead in the direction they would seem to do. What they want in utility is, however, fully made up in beauty. They are planted with trees on each side, and all objects that can be seen at a little distance are framed or buried in tree vegetation in the most singular manner.'

Jersey's lanes continue to delight and are no more narrow, sunken or difficult to negotiate than many similar ways in Devon and Cornwall.

Jersey's roads carry an astonishing volume of traffic – car ownership is amongst the highest in the world, in an island nine miles by five! In many ways, Jersey's traffic problems are a microcosm of those in all developed countries. Sometimes it seems that the car in Jersey is not so much a means of getting from A to B as a kind of fashion accessory – witness the luxury cars, suitable for long-distance driving at speeds far in excess of Jersey's 40 mph limit and, most bizarrely, the 4-wheel drive, quasi-military vehicles, scarcely necessary for commuting to and from St. Helier.

A Jersey practice which is sensible and works well is the 'Filter in Turn' system whereby, at a junction, vehicles approaching from adjacent roads take it in turn to enter the junction. The good manners of Jersey drivers ensures that this system works smoothly and results in a steady traffic flow without anyone becoming frustrated because they cannot make progress. It's unlikely it would work on the mainland where the prospect of a roundabout usually presents an opportunity for competition rather than cooperation!

*see also* GREEN LANES

## ROYAL COURT

The Royal Court of Jersey, an ancient institution dating back to 1204, is housed in a building next to the States Assembly in the Royal Square. It comprises the **Bailiff** and twelve **Jurats** and is the Island's premier court of justice. Now Jersey's principal judicial body, the Royal Court, before the ascendancy of the **States**, possessed legislative as well as judicial powers.

*see also* LAW.

## SEIGNEUR

This title originates in the feudal system introduced by the **Normans**, and refers to the person who ruled over his fief, or property granted him by the Duke of Normandy, what in England is generally referred to as the 'Lord of the Manor.' Seigneurs still exist but have little or no power, unlike the situation in the past, when the Seigneur held all kinds of privileges and had the right to hold a court for the ordering of his domain and the power to punish offenders, including the death sentence. In turn, the Seigneur had to pay service to the Duke, or Sovereign.

*see also* FEUDALISM

## SENATOR

The twelve Senators represent the most senior tier of Jersey's elected representatives. They sit in the Senate, the **States** upper chamber. Six are elected every three years by the whole electorate of the Island and when elected and sworn in they represent the whole Island. *See also* GOVERNMENT

## SHIPS AND SHIPPING

At the time of writing (1997) Jersey is reduced to reliance on one state-on-the-art catamaran, which sails only in favourable weather conditions, for links by sea with the English mainland. This seems ironic for an Island whose wealth has traditionally owed much to the sea – to fishing, privateering, smuggling, shipbuilding and trading.

In the Middle Ages fishing was an important source of income for sea-going Jerseymen and large quantities of salted conger eel were exported to the Continent. And Jerseymen were among the first to exploit the Newfoundland Fisheries and developed a huge trade in shipping salt cod to Catholic Europe where it was in demand for fast days. However, whenever war broke out, every shipowner applied for his vessel to become an auxiliary ship in the Navy. This allowed him to prowl about the Channel and prey on enemy ships – to become a privateer, i.e. a licensed pirate. Many local families accumulated fortunes in this way though the tide turned somewhat during the Napoleonic Wars when French ships were generally better armed – at this time Jersey lost some two-thirds of its shipping.

Here is a contemporary report from a guide book of 1822:

'The Newfoundland Trade is the most considerable: vessels go for the purpose of fishing on the banks, and carry with them, from Jersey, woollen manufactures of almost every kind; nets, cordage, and iron; also salt, for the curing of fish; and having obtained a cargo, either by fishing or purchase, they proceed with it to many of the ports of Spain, the Mediterranean and to both North and South America. In time of war, every one is employed in privateering and scarcely sufficient hands are left for the cultivation of the soil.'

The heyday of smuggling was during the early nineteenth century when contraband goods were loaded in Jersey and shipped to south-west England and south Wales.

The first steamship arrived in Jersey in 1823 and heralded a new era of relatively safe and reliable sea travel from England. In the meantime, Jersey continued to develop its wooden shipbuilding industry, an activity which spread from town across the beach at St. Aubin's and along Grève d'Azette; there was also a considerable industry at Gorey. By mid-nineteenth century the

ADVERTISEMENT

# GREAT WESTERN RAILWAY.

## WEYMOUTH AND CHANNEL ISLANDS'
### STEAM PACKET COMPANY LIMITED.

## STEAM COMMUNICATION
### BETWEEN

# WEYMOUTH
### AND THE

# CHANNEL ISLANDS,

(THE SHORTEST SEA PASSAGE BY THREE HOURS.)

 THE iron fast steam boats "*AQUILA*," and " *CYGNUS*," fitted up in the most splendid style, with every requisite accommodation, and making daylight passages both ways, ply FROM JERSEY TO WEYMOUTH, CALLING AT GUERNSEY, and *vice-versâ*. For Further Particulars see Time Bills.

All Goods should be addressed as follows: To Jersey or Guernsey *viâ* Weymouth per Great Western Railway and Steamer, care of Mr. Roberts, Weymouth; and to prevent delay in the Shipment of Goods, particulars of the contents and value of each Package should also be forwarded by Post to Mr. W. Roberts. Bonded or exciseable Goods cannot be shipped without such advice.

For further Particulars apply to

THOMAS RENOUF, . . . Jersey.

JOHN JONES, . . . . . Guernsey.

W. ROBERTS, . . . . . Weymouth.

Jersey fleet had grown to an astonishing 500 vessels and the Island occupied fifth place in the league table of British ports. However, the advent of the iron-hulled ship spelt the end of this boom period in Jersey's maritime past and the local shipbuilding industry declined to almost nothing in a few short years during the 1860s.

Old photographs of St. Helier Harbour reveal a forest of masts and much activity. Today, harbour facilities are expanding fast with the increase in leisure craft and the large car-carrying vessels which now service the Island. And yet, apart from the occasional ferry, the Harbour today seems curiously quiet and unpeopled, at least compared to the scene only a generation ago when cars had to be individually craned on and off, loose cargo manhandled, and farm lorries queued to deliver potatoes for export.

## SHOPS AND SHOPPING

As each year passes the number of shops in St. Helier with a local name above them grows fewer, though three of the largest retail businesses are happily still with us, *viz*. De Gruchy, Voisin and Le Gallais, all splendid emporia with their own distinctive ambience. The cloning of the town's main shopping streets continues apace, in the same way it does in almost every town on the mainland, so that any individual character is fast disappearing. Certainly the proportion of outlets selling luxury goods, like jewellery and perfume, is noticeably greater in Jersey, and there is a great variety of eating places, usually just off the main streets, though probably not more than the more prosperous towns of England.

Shopping, that great British pastime, is given plenty of opportunity with extended opening hours, which in summer often means 10pm, though the matter of Sunday opening is one which is, at the time of writing, being hotly debated, there being some way to go before 'deregulation' is as complete as the mainland.

All Jersey bibliophiles will know, and all visiting bibliophiles should know, that Thesaurus is the name of the Island's immense and highly attractive second-hand bookshop. Some 85,000 books, plus prints, maps and old postcards are housed in a spacious old property, beyond an unmodernised but beautifully restored façade; indeed, the owners, Kevin and Irene Creaton, were awarded a certificate from Save Jersey's Heritage for their efforts. The interior, even apart from the books, is a delight. One noteworthy feature is a miniature garden in the middle of the green carpeted floor, another the great brass eagle lectern which was donated by resident author Jack Higgins (of *The Eagle Has Landed* fame). Not surprisingly, Thesaurus is a Channel Islands specialist and aims to stock all new books on the archipelago, as well as a good collection of used books. The stock is extensive – for endless browsing, but well organised – so you can find what you want.

*Thesaurus, 3 Burrard Street, St. Helier, Jersey.*

## SLIP

This tiny word refers to those fine granite-built ramps which give access from the landward side of the sea wall to the beach. They are solidly constructed, with massive blocks lining the sides and stone setts laid horizontally between. The setts are ridged so as to provide a good grip for the horses which once pulled the **vraic** carts and boats up and down. Like so many other granite structures, Jersey's many slipways are a tribute to the skill and strength of those men who built them and to the enduring beauty of the native stone. They are simple, functional, built to last; they surely hold no opportunity for the property developers so should be ours to enjoy for many years to come.

## SOCIETE JERSIAISE

Like so many local antiquarian societies in mainland Britain, Jersey's own Société Jersiaise came together in the Victorian era – in 1873, perhaps a little later than most. Its objective was, and remains, to encourage 'the study of the history and the preservation of the antiquities of Jersey.'

The Société has traditionally been a great influence in Island affairs. It currently has a membership approaching 4,000 – a remarkable figure for a community the size of Jersey. Some members are active in one or more of the many special interest groups or attend  periodic lectures held by the Société. An annual Bulletin is produced which contains learned articles on particular topics and, as a whole, the Bulletin represents a considerable resource of material which would not otherwise have appeared in print.

The headquarters of the Société have always been in Pier Road, now in a recently converted building adjacent to the former Museum, which itself is now restored as an eighteenth century merchant's house. The new, award-winning Museum, opened in 1992, is in a purpose-built structure immediately behind, facing the Weighbridge. The former Museum may have been a bit of a jumble but there was something appealing and satisfying about the traditional Museum with its abundance of artefacts, lack of 'interpretation' (so that something is left to the imagination) and sheer serendipity. It also had an excellent bookshop where you could see every publication on Jersey currently in print. The new Museum is state-of-the-art, expertly presented and greatly informative. On the other hand, many feel that one visit is enough, though special exhibitions are always a temptation.

The Jersey Museums Service is funded by the States although the Société Jersiaise owns the buildings and maintains a considerable influence via the Jersey Heritage Trust. With the recent completion of the Hamptonne Museum of Rural Life and the new Maritime Museum due to open in 1997, Jersey may justly feel that now, at last, she celebrates her diverse and colourful past with professionalism and pride.

*Société Jersiaise, 7 Pier Road, St. Helier, Jersey.*

## STATES OF JERSEY

The States of Jersey refers to the Island's legislative chamber and is composed of three elements, or *états*, as follows: 12 **Senators**, voted in by an all-island electorate; 12 **Constables**, each representing a **parish**; 29 **Deputies**, each representing a parish or, in the more populous parishes, an electoral district within a parish. The President of the States is the **Bailiff**, appointed by the Crown.

The States originally consisted of 12 **Jurats**, 12 Rectors and 12 Constables, one for each 12 parishes, respectively representing the judiciary, the church and the people. The Code of 1771 finally recognised the States as the Island's sole legislative body. In 1948 the States were thoroughly reformed – Senators, elected on an island-wide franchise, replaced the Jurats; while the Rectors were replaced by more Deputies elected on a parish basis.

The Jersey States prides itself on being free of party politics, that the electors vote for the person rather than a party. This may be true but political life seems to be just as animated as it was in the days when Jersey was riven by party politics.
*see also* GOVERNMENT

## STREET NAMES in St. Helier

St. Helier's street names make an interesting study. They are, unlike their country cousins, mainly English, and reflect, by and large, the great nineteenth century urban expansion. Here are some of the town's street and place names with a note of their origins:

**Beresford Street**: Named after the last Governor of Jersey, 1821-54;

**Mount Bingham**: Named after a former Lieutenant-Governor;

**Cattle Street**: So named because it led to the former cattle market in Minden Place;

**Clarence Road**: Named after Duke of Clarence, later William IV;

**Colomberie**: derived from the colombier, meaning dovecot, which was formerly located here;

**Conway Street**: Named after Field Marshall Henry Seymour Conway, Govenor 1772-95;

**Don Street** and **Don Road**: Named after General Sir George Don;

**Elizabeth Castle**: Named after Queen Elizabeth I and formerly headquarters of the Governor of Jersey;

**Gloucester Street**: Named after the Duke of Gloucester who visited Jersey in 1817;

**Halkett Place and Halkett Street**: Named after Major General Sir Colin Halkett, Lieutenant-Governor 1821-30;

**Hilgrove Street**: Named after St. Tomkyns Hilgrove Turner, Lieutenant-Governor of Jersey 1814- 16. This thoroughfare, close by the market, became known as French Lane because it was the meeting place of Jersey's Breton seasonal workers;

**Howard Davis Park**: Presented to the Island by T.B. Davis in memory of his son Howard Davis who was killed in World War I;

**King Street**: Probably named after King George III;

**Mulcaster Street**: Named after Captain Mulcaster, the officer in command of Elizabeth Castle when the French invaded in 1781; Mulcaster was shot through the heart in the ensuing Battle of Jersey;

**The Parade**: Developed by General Don in 1811 as a parade ground. It was later converted into gardens and an impressive statue of General Don erected in 1885;

**Queen Street**: Probably named after Queen Charlotte, wife of George III;

**Raleigh Avenue**: Named after Sir Walter Raleigh, Governor 1600-03;

**Fort Regent**: Town Hill was purchased by the British Government in order to build a fort; it was named after the

Prince Regent, later King George IV;

**Victoria** ... Queen Victoria gave her name to Victoria Avenue, Victoria College, Victoria Harbour, two Victoria Towers (in St. Helier and St. Martin) and also to Queen's Road and Queen's Valley;

**Weighbridge**: So named because the public weighbridge was located there from 1825 to 1970;

**York Street**: Named after Duke of York, brother of William IV.

## SURNAMES

An easily applied, though unscientific, survey of the most commonly occurring local names may be carried out by examining the Jersey Telephone Directory. A cursory inspection of the current edition reveals the following, in order of frequency – the number to the right of each name denotes the number of column centimeters occupied by each name:

| | | | |
|---|---|---|---|
| De La Haye | 46 | Le Sueur | 27 |
| De Gruchy | 45 | Le Maistre | 27 |
| Bisson | 44 | Amy | 26 |
| Renouf | 44 | Mauger | 26 |
| Le Marquand | 42 | Blampied | 25 |
| Le Cornu | 39 | Le Quesne | 25 |
| Vibert | 38 | Marett | 25 |
| Gallichan | 36 | Romeril | 25 |
| Pallot | 36 | Perchard | 25 |
| Hamon | 35 | Luce | 23 |
| Baudains | 32 | Du Feu | 22 |
| Le Feuvre/Fevre | 32 | Coutanche | 22 |
| Falle | 31 | Rondel | 22 |
| Noel | 31 | Michel | 21 |
| Huelin | 27 | Queree | 20 |
| Le Brocq | 27 | Syvret | 20 |

It is interesting to note that each of the two commonest English names – Smith and Jones – far outstrips even the most frequently occurring Jersey name, with 86 and 56 column centimeters respectively. Even Taylor has 52!

Yet Jersey surnames remain among the most visible and uniquely identifying features of the Island, especially those prefixed with 'Le'. Many Jersey businesses, particularly those catering for the necessities of life, are old established and commonly bear local names. Raoul Lemprière, in his book *The Channel Islands*, makes the point that particular names are often associated with Jersey, and may be absent or spelt differently in the other islands. He suggests that over 450 surnames have been known since the sixteenth century.

Many Jersey names have become extinct in Jersey but may flourish abroad, intermarriage and emigration being the cause. The great Jersey diaspora would make a fascinating study – wherever Jersey ships sailed, at the very least, then Jersey folk are likely to have settled.

# T

## TAPESTRY

The notion of creating a tapestry to commemorate the 50th Anniversary of the Liberation in 1995 was first mooted in 1988. Wayne Audrain, of Jersey Museum, established the design and each of Jersey's twelve parishes undertook a panel (each measuring 6 x 3 feet). As a whole, the tapestry tells the story of the war years from the outbreak of war, through the Occupation to eventual Liberation. This ambitious community project took seven years and 7,500,000 stiches to complete. It now has a permanent home at the Harbour next to the Maritime Museum.

## TIDE

Because of its position in the eye of the Bay of Mont St. Michel, the coasts of Jersey enjoy some of the largest tidal movements anywhere in the world. You can expect spring tides of 38 or even 40 feet. Low pressure, a stiff on-shore wind and a spring tide can result in the flooding of low-lying areas while, at some places, the sea seems to vanish altogether at low tide. If you walk out to meet low tide at the Dicq, for example, you will see it advancing across the flat sands at a steady creep. Great care must be taken if you venture out onto rocks anywhere in Jersey when the tide is rising, but especially from Grève d'Azette, right around to Grouville. The sea sweeps along the sandy channels between the rocky outcrops with tremendous power, and makes wading in the current exceedingly difficult.

About 17 square miles of temporary land around Jersey is exposed at low tide, almost half as much again as the permanent area of the Island. One consequence of this huge movement of water is that Jersey enjoys an extensive littoral zone (the bit between high and low water) which supports a rich habitat for a range of specially adapted plants and animals.

This twice-daily spectacle of the rise and fall of the sea provides a stunning piece of natural theatre. How many times does one overhear visitors remark on it as they gaze seaward from the bus as it heads across St. Aubin's Bay. A taxi driver once remarked, with a completely straight face, that the previous week there had been such a low tide that people had walked across to France! That may once have been possible, but not since the end of the last Ice Age.

By contrast to the seas around Jersey, the Mediterranean seems all wrong – no tide to provide a natural beach-cleaning service, no changing view of the beach, no rock pools filled and refilled twice daily: really rather boring in comparison.

**TOURISM**

Britain's first tourists were possibly those persons from wealthy families, during the eighteenth century, who embarked on the so-called Grand Tour. This consisted of a round of visits to the art treasures and watering places of civilised Europe – the emphasis on sight-seeing, art and architecture; Italy was the most favoured destination, though several countries were normally included in such a tour.

The Channel Islands were never regarded as worthy of inclusion though, by the end of the eighteenth century, a few curious travellers were finding their way here. The ending of the protracted Napoleonic Wars in 1815 rendered the sea crossing a good deal less hazardous and this served to encourage a steady growth in the number of tourists.

Geroge Eliot, one of England's greatest novelists, now perhaps best known as the author of *Middlemarch*, visited Jersey in 1857, arriving from the Isles of Scilly on 12th May. She loved Jersey from the outset and compared it favourably with the Scillies:

'It was a beautiful moment ... when we came to our lodgings at Gorey. The orchards were all in blossom – and this is an island of orchards. They cover the slopes; they stretch before you in shady, grassy, indefinite extent through every other gateway by the roadside, they flourish in some spots almost close to the sea. What a contrast to the Scilly Isles!'

She was soon to discover Queen's Valley, long before it became a reservoir:

'The first lovely walk we found inland was the Queen's Fern Valley, where a broad strip of meadow and pasture lies between two high slopes covered with woods and ferny wilderness ... Everywhere there are tethered cows, looking at you with meek faces – mild eyed, sleek, fawn-coloured creatures, with delicate downy udders.'

One final sentence which sums up Miss Eliot's pleasure at discovering Jersey, and a quote which could have provided Tourism with a fine piece of advertising copy aimed at Victorian travellers:

'The island is one labyrinth of delicious roads and lanes, leading you by the most charming nooks of houses with shady grounds and shrubbiness – delightful farm homesteads – and trim villas.'

Sailing ships soon gave way to steam and this greatly improved the reliability of the sea crossing; more hotels opened, many of which were founded by French immigrants. David Ansted reported in 1862:

'There is a rapid increase in the number of tourists who flock over by hundreds, in search of health, amusement, and relaxation; and who find their time well spent in examining the numerous objects of interest that here abound.'

*An early tourist gazing in awe at a cromlech or, as the old guide books describe it, 'Druid Stones'.*

Those 'numerous objects of interest' formed the stuff of the sightseeeing tour and this is elaborated upon under the heading of GUIDE BOOKS. Of the tour itself, these eventually became less dependent upon individual enterprise and more in the control of local operators with, according to some observers, definite advantages; the following extract is taken from a guide book published in 1882:

'The Excursion cars are an institution in Jersey; they are interesting in themselves, for the study of character afforded by meeting such miscellaneous groups of people. Then the height of the cars allows you to see over the highest fences, which you cannot do when in an ordinary carriage or on foot, and the exhilarating experience of passing rapidly through a beautiful country, breathing the pure air of these islands and viewing the most lovely scenery is to most people a novel experience.'

Apart from sight-seeing, swimming grew in popularity throughout the nineteenth century. Here, writing in 1862, is Octavius Rooke, who otherwise betrays a rather arrogant and cynical attitude towards Jersey and her inhabitants, enthusing about the glories of sea bathing at Bouley Bay:

'Let us go beyond the curious rock where the sea creams with freshness. Far down through the deep wave we catch the glitter of the bright round stones, and plunging in, the water seethes around us, and splash the waters high, which glisten in the air and then descend in spray. A whole year's toil seems washed away, and as we don our habiliments upon the rocks our minds and bodies feel alike elastic.'

By the outbreak of the First World War, the number of summer tourists had grown to 70,000 and, between the wars, the numbers doubled. Jersey was well suited to appeal to the passion for swimming and the open air which prevailed in the inter-war years (the bathing beauties on the cover of this book are from a Jersey guide for tourists published in 1936).

It goes without saying that the German Occupation in 1940 caused an abrupt end to tourism but, once peace had been restored, the industry made a rapid recovery. By 1949 there were 250,000 visitors of whom 76,000 arrived by air. Jersey was becoming a popular destination in every sense. Popular because of its beauties and duty-free status, but popular because the cost of a holiday here was within the reach of the ordinary family.

In 1953, the travel writer S.P.B. Mais spent a fortnight in the Channel Islands and, trying his utmost to reflect the democratic spirit which prevailed in those post-war years, wrote as follows:

'The Island of Jersey has indeed reached a high degree of efficiency in the organisation of enjoyable holidays, with a large variety of coach tours and excursions and, for those whose age demands that form of diversion, evening outings, all within the reach of the poorest of us.

If I have heard a criticism about Jersey voiced, though it is not one which I have to complain of myself, it is to the effect that not every visitor to these lovely parts wishes to be regaled with the strains of the rumba and the samba until midnight or 1 a.m.'

The heyday of the organised coach tour was in the 1950s and Crazy Nite (sic) was a mainstay of any coach company's programme, a typical venue for which was the Château Plaisir on the Five Mile Road. The most popular afternoon trip was the Coastal Tour – a 40 mile drive for 5 shillings. The coach driver's commentary was often humorous and hyperbolic. For example, when passing a field of tomatoes tied to wooden crosses visitors would be offered the explanation that they were looking at a tomato cemetery, that burying dead tomatoes was an old Jersey custom, and that each one had its own cross. It was extraordinary how many seemed to believe that story.

Apart from the Coastal Tour there was the Afternoon Tour which called at the Occupation Museum (at Hougue Bie), the Glass Church and the Underground Hospital. In the 1950s, these destinations comprised the sum total of Jersey's visitor attractions. How different the situation is today when the visitor is hard put to visit every worthwhile attraction in a fortnight's holiday, even taking in two venues each day.

Self-drive hire cars eroded the business of the coach tour operators, especially through the 1960s and 70s, so that the once numerous coach companies have been largely replaced by a range of car hire firms. And today a growing number of 'Green Tourists' demand bicycles and footpaths rather than cars.

Tourism grew throughout the 1950s, 60s and 70s overtaking agriculture as the prime source of wealth. It peaked around 1990, since when the number of visitor beds has been in steady decline, with a knock-on effect throughout the service sector. Competition, first from Mediterranean resorts and latterly from throughout the world, together with the high cost of travelling to the Island, has knocked Jersey from its perch. This has not been such a disaster for Jersey because of the enormous development of the finance industry over the past two decades.

There would appear to be some confusion in the authorities' latest attempts to market the island with the Lillie the Cow character and plans for moulding St. Helier into the image of a French town rather than developing it as the Island's own capital. Jersey, with its undoubted natural attributes – coast, country, flora and fauna, sea life, as well as history and heritage, would seem to offer a great deal for the 'Green Tourist' but this aspect of the Island sits uneasily with the fact of the Island's huge volume of traffic and the domination of St. Helier by the finance industry.

# TOWN

As it is Jersey's only real conurbation, St. Helier is universally known as 'town'. On buses you never ask for a ticket to St. Helier, always one to town. Much of St. Helier lies on the flat, having been built on marshy ground where several streams drain the surrounding hills to flow seaward. St. Aubin was at one time the more significant place in terms of trade and commerce, its harbour predating that of St. Helier, though it was long of secondary importance to St. Peter Port in Guernsey, which, compared to Jersey, provided a safe haven closer to the main trade routes.

However, with the ending of the Napoleonic Wars and the development of its own spacious harbour, St. Helier was set on a course of steady growth and development. The 'New Town', as it became known, consisting mainly of substantial houses, sometimes detached but more often in fine terraces and crescents, spread out in all directions from the old heart of town centred around the Royal Square, which traditionally had been the market place. Once the flat land had been built upon, new developments, like Almorah Crescent, began to climb the hillsides.

St. Helier today is not without charm though it cannot be claimed that it is the most attractive town in the Channel Islands. We must, grudgingly perhaps, pass this accolade to St. Peter Port, whose pleasing mixture of buildings which, by and large, seem to maintain a similar modest scale, tumble down the hill towards its impressive harbours, and enjoy a wide view towards smaller Channel Islands nearby. And let us not forget St. Anne's, in Alderney, which has all the appeal of an unspoilt version of a typical Cornish seaside town.

Apart from the fact that much of St. Helier is on the flat, the town's development during the nineteenth century lay in the

*Opposite: Plan of St. Helier which was reproduced in Stead's book published in 1809, before the great expansion of the town which began in the following decade and continued throughout the century.*

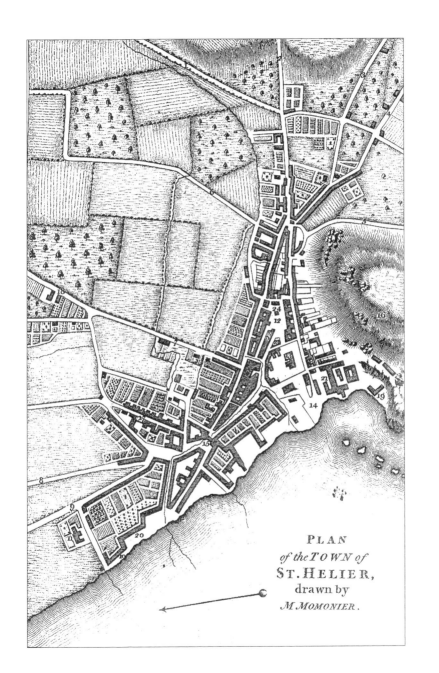

PLAN
of the TOWN of
ST. HELIER,
drawn by
M. MOMONIER.

hands of speculative builders whose aim was to pack in as many dwellings as possible, with little regard for fine vistas – tree-lined streets, for instance, or the provision of open spaces, such as squares and parks. The exceptions, like The Parade, Howard Davis Park and People's Park are doubly welcome.

The piecemeal development of St. Helier began in earnest in the 1960s and continues apace. Some of the more recent development is much more acceptable – either proudly contemporary, like the Royal Bank of Scotland building on the corner of Bath Street and Phillips Street, or modestly in the Jersey vernacular tradition, with windows and rooflines to match. Better this than mock-Georgian or monstrosities like the red-brick canyons of the offices erected on the old Forum Cinema site. Perhaps the greatest outrage have been the multi-storey car parks which have all the charm one might expect of aliens from outer space. It may not be possible to design such apparently necessary structures more fittingly, but the Sand Street multi-storey, for example, looks like a Gulliver in Lilliput.

With the influx of English residents, mainly to St. Helier, during the nineteenth century, and the burgeoning trade and commerce centred in the town and around the harbour, Jersey's capital became identified with the English tongue and sophisticated ways as opposed to the country, where Jersey-French still held sway and a traditional way of life survived. Not surprisingly, perhaps, there arose a considerable rivalry between town and country. Some Jersey folk will recall the nicknames 'Town Pat' and 'Country Johnny', the latter deriving from 'Jeannots', the word used to denote natives of St. John, regarded as a far cry, both geographically and culturally, from the inhabitants of St. Helier. Raoul Lemprière records that the country people knew the townsfolk as 'Les clyichards', a Jersey-French expression meaning 'those suffering from diarrhoea', or 'palefaces'.

*see also* STREET NAMES

# V

## VERGEE

The Jersey vergée is a measure of land area: 2.25 vergées are equivalent to 1 English acre (as opposed to 2.5 Guernsey vergées).

## VICTORIA COLLEGE

Jersey's premier independent school is centred on a fine Victorian building, looking like a cross between a church and a castle, which occupies an elevated position to the east of St. Helier. In was in 1846, when Queen Victoria visited the Island, that the idea arose of building the school, as a means of commemorating her visit; it was opened in 1852. Many of Jersey's finest have graduated from Victoria College. It is a boys' day public school and caters for 620 boys from 11 to 18.

## VINGTAINE

Each of Jersey's twelve parishes is divided into a number of *vingtaines* (except St. Ouen, which is divided into *cueillettes*) which are responsible for the collection of the parish rate.

## VINGTENIER

Like the **centenier**, a parochial officer. Each **parish** has a number of elected vingteniers who assist the centeniers and the **Constable** in their police work and who are responsible for the collection of the parish rate. The Vingtenier is so called because, originally, he was responsible for twenty families.

## 'VISITORS'

is the rather charming epithet traditionally used in Jersey to refer to the large numbers of people, mainly British, who choose to spend their holidays in the Island. How much more affectionate than the anonymous 'Tourist', or the rather derogatory 'grockle', so ubiquitously quoted in Devon and Cornwall and featured on the elitist bumper sticker, 'I'm not a grockle, I live here.'   'Visitors' conjures up the notion of an invitation, of friends coming round on a Sunday afternoon.

## VRAIC

(pronounced 'rack') is the Jersey-French word for seaweed still in common usage by Islanders today. *Vraic* is collected from the beaches to be used as fertiliser on Jersey's fields, where it enriches the soil, particularly in the sandy western parishes. *Vraic* is used fresh, when it is spread directly on to the fields, and formerly as ash after burning, when its valuable mineral content is present in more concentrated form. Burning was traditionally carried out at St. Ouen's; the illustration and caption reproduced below is from a guide book (*The Channel Islands* by Octavius Rooke) published in 1856:

Rooke's caption reads as follows: *'Under the cliffs which form the headland of Le Tacq nestles a village, with wreaths of white smoke ascending from the chimneys, caused by the large fires they keep up to reduce to ashes the vraic before they put it on the land.'*

And here is David Ansted, in the mid-nineteenth century, describing *vraic* and the process of *vraicing:*

'Seaweed, when cut, is either thickly spread on the land and ploughed in fresh with a deep plough, or dried on the beach and burnt on the cottagers' hearths as fuel, certainly not on account of the cheerful appearance of the fire or its pleasant odour, but because the charred ash thus produced sells at a good price for manure. The fire smoulders quietly; it is never extinguished, but constantly renewed, and the whitest of all smoke ascends night and day from the rude chimneys of these humble dwellings.

Vraicing is a custom that time has hallowed into an institution ... the cutting of the vraic (vraic scie) is the occasion of a general holiday. Large parties grouped into sets of two or three families resort to the most promising places, where the weed is thickest and longest, and cut it with a small kind of reaping-hook, throwing it into heaps till the tide flows. It is then carried out of reach of the advancing tide as far as possible. In the evening, after the day's work, the parties meet at some neighbouring house of refreshment. The evening closes with a dance.

The bringing in of the vraic venant, allowed to all persons from sunrise to sunset, all the year round, is also a striking and pleasing sight. At sunset, after a gale, when the tide is out, the carts are drawn up, and the men stationed along the shore, prepared to rake in all that can be got, each man provided with an immense rake, with a head two or three feet wide and teeth a foot long, and the handle a young tree from 12 to 18 feet in length.'

Professional vraicers also once existed, though the *vraicing* season was more often an opportunity for family and friends to work together to ensure a good harvest. Because it was such a valuable harvest, the gathering of the *vraic scie* was strictly controlled by law.

*Vraic* is still gathered and tractors and lorries may be seen engaged upon the task at various spots around the coast, but gone are the days when seaweed was stacked like hay to dry beside the Five Mile Road.

Whilst on the indelicate but essential subject of manure, Mr. Ansted, with Victorian decorum, also notes the following:

> 'In Jersey, the human population being extremely large in proportion to the area of cultivated land, the quantity of other kinds of manure is excessive, and for the most part good use is made of it.'

# W

## WATERMILLS

Much of Jersey's limited rainfall drains away on the surface, the water collecting in streams which flow seaward. In former times, every opportunity was taken to utilise this movement to turn machinery for grinding corn and other purposes. Because Jersey is essentially a plateau tilted to the south, several of the larger streams flow into St. Aubin's Bay. Waterworks Valley, or Rue des Moulins, once supported no fewer than seven watermills.

Watermills were in operation from medieval times, when they belonged to the **Seigneurs**. There are no working mills today – the last were working in the nineteenth century though one or two were pressed into service during the Occupation . However, Moulin de Quetivel has been lovingly restored by the National Trust for Jersey and is put into operation from time to time. In 1996 the Trust acquired the impressive Tesson Mill, just down the valley. It is possible to follow a footpath beside the mill leat between these two former mills. Another fascinating site may be seen at Moulin de Lecq, the pub at Grève de Lecq, where an overshot water-wheel is fed from a leat which follows the hillside above and turns machinery behind the ground floor bar.

## WINDMILLS

Surrounded by the open sea, a steady wind quite often blows across Jersey; a number of windmills were built from medieval times onwards to take advantage of this gift of nature in those parts of the Island far from a stream and the possibility of water power. The best preserved has been redeveloped into the Windmill Inn at St. Peter. The stone structure of Grantez Windmill still looks out over St. Ouen's Bay. Other survivors are Le Moulin de Grouville in Grouville and Le Moulin de Rozel in St. Martin.

## Jersey WONDERS

or *Des Mèrvelles*, are a variety of doughnut and consist of flour, sugar, butter, salt, lemon juice and nutmeg. The mixture is divided into walnut-sized balls, rolled into rectangular shapes into which three cuts are made through the centre. The ends are passed under and up through the central slit, crossing one through the other. It is this simple but original twist which is the Jersey Wonder's special characteristic. They are deep-fried in fat until golden-brown and are best consumed while still fresh and hot. There is a tradition that Wonders should only be cooked when the tide is going out: a rising tide will cause the fat to boil over.

## ZOO

This book has deliberately steered clear of tourist attractions but ZOO is included for two reaons. Firstly, Jersey Zoo is much more than simply a tourist attraction, and secondly, the temptation to end a Jersey Alphabet with an entry for Z is irresistible.

Jersey Zoo is renowned for its work with endangered species. It was founded in 1958 by the late Gerald Durrell as the Jersey Zoological Park at Les Augrès Manor in Trinity. Subsequently in 1963 the Jersey Preservation Trust was created with the aim of eventually returning species faced with extinction to their native breeding places.

# Useful Reading

Listed below are books referred to in the text or otherwise recommended. All Seaflower titles of Jersey interest are listed separately on the two pages following this list.

ANSTED, David Thomas: *The Channel Islands*, 1862.
ASHWORTH: *Historic Jersey, the Parishes and Commerce*, 1993.
BACKHURST, Marie-Louise: *Family History in Jersey*, 1991.
BALLEINE, G.R.: *The Bailiwick of Jersey*, 1951.
BALLEINE, G.R.: *Balleine's History of Jersey* (revised and enlarged by Marguerite Syvret and Joan Stevens), 1981.
BISSON, Sidney: *Jersey our Island*, 1950.
BOIS, Elizabeth et al: *Jersey Through the Lens Again*, 1989.
BRANTHWAITE, Jasper and MACLEAN, Frank: *Two Knapsacks in the Channel Islands*, c. 1890.
*BRITISH GEOLOGICAL SURVEY: JERSEY*, 1989.
BUNTING, Madeleine: *The Model Occupation*, 1995.
CAREY, Edith F.: *The Channel Islands*, 1904.
CHISHOLM, Cecil: *Retire to the Sun*, 1961.
COLEMAN, Tessa: *Threads of History: the Jersey Occupation Tapestry*, 1995.
COYSH. Victor (ed.): *The Channel Islands, a new study*, 1977.
CROSS, Amanda: *Tastes of the Channel Isles*, 1983.
HOLLAND, Clive: *Things seen in the Channel Islands*, c. 1950.
HOOKE, Winifred D.: *The Channel Islands*, 1953.
INGLIS, Henry D.: *The Channel Islands*, 1834.
JEAN, John: *Jersey Sailing Ships*, 1982.
JEE, Nigel: *Landscape of the Channel Islands*, 1982.
LE SUEUR, Frances: *A Natural History of Jersey*, 1976.
LEMPRIERE, RAOUL: *Buildings and Memorials of the Channel Islands*, 1980.
LEMPRIERE, RAOUL: *Customs, Ceremonies and Traditions of the Channel Islands*, 1976.
LEMPRIERE, RAOUL: *Portrait of the Channel Islands*, 1970.
LOCKLEY, R.M.: *The Charm of the Channel Islands*, 1950.
MAIS, S.P.B.: *The Channel Islands*, 1953.
MAUGHAM, R.C.F.: *The Island of Jersey Today*, 1939.
MAYNE, Richard et al: *Jersey Through the Lens*, 1975.
NETTLES, John: *Bergerac's Jersey*, 1988.

NETTLES, John: *John Nettles' Jersey*, 1992.
ROOKE, Octavius: *The Channel Islands*, 1856.
STEAD, J.: *A Picture of Jersey, or Stranger's Companion through that Island* (published in Jersey), 1809.
STEVENS, Joan: *Old Jersey Houses Vol. 1*, 1965.
STEVENS, Joan: *Old Jersey Houses Vol. 2*, 1977.
SYVRET, Marguerite: *Edmund Blampied*, 1986.
UTTLEY, JOHN: *The Story of the Channel Islands*, 1966.
VON AUFSESS: *Occupation Diary*,
WYATT, Horace: *Jersey in Jail 1940-45* (Illustrated by Edmund Blampied), 1945.
*The Channel Islands and Islanders* by DFS (published in Ediburgh), 1882.
*Letters from Jersey* (published jointly in Cambridge and Jersey) 1830.
*Jersey Place Names*, 1986.
*Jersey's Lost Heritage*, 1996.
*Queen of the Isles*, 1840.
*Stranger's Guide to Jersey* (published in Guernsey), 1822.
*A Week's Visit to Jersey* (published in Jersey), 1844.

## Source of the Illustrations:

Cover, frontispiece, page 76 – *Sunny Jersey: Official Island Guide*, c. 1936.
Page 9 – John Le Dain: *Jersey Rambles*, 1992.
Page 23 – The Traveller's Companion Series: *London to the Channel Islands*, 1890.
Page 29, 74, 112, 120 – Octavius Rooke: *The Channel Islands*, 1856.
Page 31 – Rev. Edward Durell: *The Picturesque and Historical Guide to the Island of Jersey*, 1847.
Page 36, 40, 41 – *Chambers Encyclopaedia*.
Page 39, 91 – Jasper Branthwaite and Frank Maclean: *Two Knapsacks in the Channel Islands*, c. 1890.
Page 44 – *The Channel Islands* (Ward Lock Guide Book), c. 1936.
Page 60 – *Views of Jersey*, 1858-68.
Page 84 – Wood engraving by Thomas Bewick.
Page 101 – *Thorne's Guide to Jersey* (published in Jersey), 1857.
Page 115 – *Jersey Chamber of Commerce Guide Book*, 1953.
Page 117 – J. Stead: *A Picture of Jersey, or Stranger's Companion through that Island* (published in Jersey), 1809.

# The *Jersey Collection* from SEAFLOWER BOOKS:

## WILD ISLAND: *Jersey Nature Diary*
by Peter Double and Nick Parlett
*119 pages; 100 illustrations; Price £7.95*

## JERSEY WEATHER AND TIDES
by Peter Manton
*95 pages; Illustrated throughout; Price £5.95*

## THE MOTOR CAR IN JERSEY
*by David Scott Warren*
*127 pages; Illustrated; Price £6.95*

## JERSEY OCCUPATION DIARY
*Her Story of the German Occupation, 1940-45*
by Nan Le Ruez
*302 pages; Illustrated with original pencil drawings,*
*photographs and map; Price £9.95*

## JERSEY IN LONDON
*A History of the Jersey Society in London, 1896-1989*
by Brian Ahier Read
*191 pages; illustrated; Price £6.95*

## JERSEY: NOT QUITE BRITISH
*The Rural History of a Singular People*
by David Le Feuvre
*159 pages; original illustrations; Price £5.95*

## THE JERSEY LILY: *The Life and Times of Lillie Langtry*
*126 pages; illustrated throughout; Price £4.95*

## JERSEY RAMBLES: *Coast and Country*
by John Le Dain
*127 pages; Pen & ink drawings & 28 maps; Price £4.95*

*Also available:*

## THE SEA WAS THEIR FORTUNE:
*A Maritime History of the Channel Islands*
by Roy McLoughlin
*160 pages; Illustrated throughout; Price £5.95*

## NO CAUSE FOR PANIC
*Channel Islands Refugees, 1940-45*
by Brian Ahier Read
*159 pages; Fully illustrated; Price £6.95*

## LIFE ON SARK
*Through the year with*
Jennifer Cochrane
*127 pages; Illustrated with photographs, pencil drawings and map; Price £4.95*

**SEAFLOWER BOOKS** may be obtained through your local
bookshop or direct from the publishers, post-free,
on receipt of net price, at:

1 The Shambles
Bradford on Avon
Wiltshire
BA15 1JS

Tel/Fax 01225 863595

Please ask for a copy of our complete illustrated list of books.